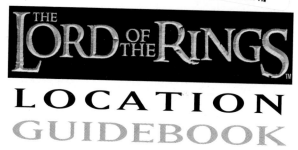

LOCATION
GUIDEBOOK

IAN BRODIE

HarperCollins*Publishers*

The author and publisher wish to thank the following
publications for their kind permission to use the
quotations appearing on these pages: *Pavement Magazine*
(pages 44, 45, 78 and 92); *The Lord of the Rings Official
Movie Guide*, by Brian Sibley (pages 20, 21, 33, 84 and
91); the *Lord of the Rings Official Fan Club Magazine*
(pages 83 and 92).

National Library of New Zealand Cataloguing-in-Publication Data

Brodie, Ian, 1957-
The Lord of the rings location guidebook / Ian Brodie.
Includes index.
ISBN 1-86950-452-6
1. Motion picture locations—New Zealand—Guidebooks. 2. Lord of the
rings, the fellowship of the ring (Motion picture) 2. Lord of the rings, the two
towers (Motion picture) 3. Lord of the rings, the return of the king (Motion
picture) 4. New Zealand—Guidebooks. I. Tolkien, J. R. R. (John Ronald
Reuel), 1892-1973. Lord of the rings. II. Title.
919.30404—dc 21

First published 2002
Reprinted 2002
HarperCollins*Publishers (New Zealand) Limited*
P.O. Box 1, Auckland

Front cover photo © New Line Productions; back cover photos: top ©
Destination Lake Taupo; centre: far left © Pierre Vinet/New Line Productions,
centre left © Dart River Jetboat Safaris, centre right © Pierre Vinet/New Line
Productions, far right ©Destination Queenstown; bottom © Pierre Vinet/New
Line Productions; photo page 2–3 © Chris Coad/New Line Productions

Designed by Dexter Fry
Typeset by Graeme Leather
Printed by Brebner, Auckland on 130 gsm matt art

This book has only been possible through the help and support of many people and organisations. I would particularly like to thank Claire Raskind-Cooper — were it not for her support and enthusiasm the project would never have proceeded. Peter Jackson, Alan Lee, Viggo Mortensen, Jan Blenkin, Erin O'Donnell, Heather Patterson, Melissa Booth, Robin Murphy and the other members of the LOTR crew provided considerable help and suggestions, and Jane Dent and Anita Bhatnagar

PIERRE VINET

from Tourism New Zealand worked tirelessly to help the book reach fruition. Special thanks are also due to Producers Barrie M. Osbourne and Fran Walsh.

One of the many joys in completing this manuscript has been the totally enthusiastic people met on the road. Their local knowledge and expertise have helped me to understand the many and varied landscapes of New Zealand as well as allowing me to add many personal anecdotes within the pages. Thanks to Michael Stearne, Alfie Speight and Barbara Swan, John Von Tunzelman, Keith Falconer, Jill Herron, Dean Alexander, Hillary Finnie, 'Scottie', Paul Eames, Paul Lambert and Bill Reid. My thanks also to the staff of all the Regional Tourism Organisations in New Zealand I pestered for information, who were so quick to offer their help.

The use of modern technology has allowed this book to be compiled 'on the fly' in some unusual locations. Thanks to Anton Napier (Philips), Bryan Morton (Computerland), Ken Goody (Kodak) for photographic support, Thomas Electronics (GPS) and Topo Map World (Electronic Maps).

Thanks also to Brian Sibley, author of the *Official Movie Guide*, and Bernard McDonald, Editor of *Pavement Magazine*, for their kind permission to use quotes from their interviews with the cast and crew.

My wife, Dianne, and children, Travis and Sally-Anne, have coped with months of The Lord of the Rings — thanks. Jane Johnson, Lorain Day and Sue Page at HarperCollins*Publishers* have calmly coped with my many queries and requests for information, and Chris Winitana wrote a superb introduction.

This book is dedicated to J.R.R. Tolkien for his vision and Peter Jackson for making this vision three-dimensional.

Ian Brodie
Wanaka 2002

Foreword

PIERRE VINET

Eighteen years old and reading J.R.R. Tolkien for the first time, I was sitting on a train as it left Wellington and rumbled up through the North Island. During the twelve-hour journey, I'd lift my eyes from the book and look at the familiar landscape — which all of a sudden looked like Middle-earth. That was over twenty years ago. Since then this story has ceased to exist for me as a work of fiction, instead it has become an account of an extraordinary passage of time. Tolkien's Middle-earth is based on a detailed mythical prehistory of this planet as it was about 6000 or 7000 years ago. For me, it reads more like history than fantasy, a fully developed society and environment the records have since forgotten.

Bringing that world to life has been a fantastic and incredibly difficult journey, but one made special because of the people and places of New Zealand. There was never any question the film wouldn't be made here. With the variety of landscapes of such an awesome nature, and the opportunity to involve talented Kiwis in a major production, it was the only way to go.

After three years of planning, on 11 October 1999, myself and a dedicated cast and crew of over 2500 people began our cinematic journey. We wanted the Middle-earth the viewer saw to feel believable and it was fantastic having Tolkien's richly created world to research all the detail. I went back and re-read particular scenes to get the image right before we started filming.

The Waikato farming country where we created Hobbiton was a like a slice of ancient England. I knew Hobbiton needed to be warm, comfortable and feel lived in. By letting the weeds grow through the cracks and establishing hedges and little gardens a year before filming, we ended up with an incredibly real place, not just a film set. It felt as if you could open the circular green door of Bag End and find Bilbo Baggins inside. Whakapapa Ski Field's rocky escarpment was the complete opposite. From one extreme to another — here the barren and inhospitable landscape was already the perfect embodiment of Mordor.

Tolkien's world was one of deep hidden valleys, barren wastelands, remote mystical mountains and lush, low valleys, and we found all these places

throughout New Zealand. Many were only accessible by helicopter and getting crew in and out wasn't easy. On reflection, I can see it had a hidden benefit — the hardships imposed by difficult country and challenging weather probably gave the actors and crew a strong sense of the reality of the characters' journey through Middle-earth. We took risks with the weather, shooting in extreme environments, such as Mt Ruapehu, Lake Mavora, Kaitoke Regional Park, Mt Cook and Mt Olympus — the landscape and raw beauty of these places were ideal for the story.

Standing at any of the 100 locations, watching Tolkien's characters come to life before my eyes, has been one of the real pleasures of my experience as director, writer and producer. The opportunity to helm a project of this size, scope and grandeur has been a once-in-a-lifetime experience, something that eighteen-year-old on the train never imagined.

Most of the crew were new to this kind of project. Their hard work and enthusiasm, combined with fantastic locations and computer enhancement technology all came together in a special way which gives our movies a unique feel — different from the Hollywood blockbusters we're used to seeing. With the help of this guidebook Tolkien fans, for whom the films were made, can experience their own unique insight into the magic and complexity of Middle-earth, and the adventure we had in order to bring it to life. My only gripe is that this book didn't exist when we started — it would have saved a huge amount of location hunting!

Peter Jackson

Contents

Acknowledgements 5

Foreword 6

Introduction to New Zealand's mythology 10

Middle-earth in New Zealand 12

NORTH ISLAND

Matamata — *Hobbiton* 17

Central North Island locations 20

Tongariro National Park — *Mordor* 22

Whakapapa Ski Field — *Mordor* 23

Tongariro Crossing — *Plains of Gorgoroth* 24

Ohakune — *Ithilien Camp* 25

Rangitikei River Gorge — *River Anduin* 26

Waitarere Forest — *Trollshaw Forest and Osgiliath Wood* 27

Otaki and Otaki Gorge — *Leaving the Shire* 28

Wellington region and locations 30

Featherston — an introduction 34

Fernside — *Lothlórien and the Gladden Fields* 36

Upper Hutt — an introduction 37

Kaitoke Regional Park — *Rivendell and the Fords of Isen* 38

Harcourt Park — *Isengard Gardens and the Orc Tree* 39

Hutt River — *River Anduin* 41

Wellington — a day tour 42

Wellington cafés and entertainment 43

The sets — *Bree and Helm's Deep* 44

SOUTH ISLAND

Nelson — an introduction 46

Takaka Hill — *Chetwood Forest* 48

Mt Olympus — *south of Rivendell* 49

Mt Owen — *Dimrill Dale* 51

Erewhon — an introduction 53

Mt Potts Station — *Edoras* 54

Tarras — *the flight to the ford* 56

Wanaka — *south of Rivendell / Misty Mountains* 57

Crown Range route to Queenstown 58

Kawarau River — *Pillars of the Kings* 61

Arrowtown — *The Ford of Bruinen* 63

Skippers Canyon — *The Ford of Bruinen* 65

Queenstown 66

Deer Park Heights 68

The Remarkables — *Dimrill Dale* 69

Queenstown to Glenorchy 71

Closeburn — *Amon Hen* 72

Twelve Mile Delta — *Ithilien Camp* 73

Glenorchy — an introduction 74

Queenstown day tour 78

Mavora Lakes — *Fangorn Forest and Nen Hithoel* 79

Mararoa River— *Silverlode River* 81

Te Anau— an introduction 82

Takaro Road — *Fangorn Forest* 83

Waiau River and Kepler Track — *River Anduin* 84

Lake Manapouri and Doubtful Sound 85

Norwest Lakes — *south of Rivendell and flight to the ford* 86

Central Otago — an introduction 88

Ida Valley — *Rohan* 89

Poolburn — *Rohan* 90

A New Zealand tour 91

Index 93

Introduction

Before the beginning there alone was Io, Io-the-parentless, Io-the-endless, Io-the-timeless, Io-without-limit.

He moved and the Great Nothingness was born. In the spiralling currents it followed itself and searched. It found heart and became ignited. It thought as does a mind. And desired as does a dream. It took form and breathed. And in a second that was a million years, it multiplied and grew. To become a shadow. A darkness. A night. A night of gestation. A night for bearing the Ancients.

There was Ranginui, the virile male, sky-bound and active. There was Papatuanuku, the female, land-bound and passive. They breathed together as lovers and in the Night-that-knows-no-end there was born to them seventy mighty sons. There was Whiro-the-dominant whose wrath was as an axe upon the tree, and Tawhiri-of-the-elements, whose breath was the wind itself. There was Tangaroa-of-the-seas, whose ceaseless waves would chisel away the land. There was Tu-of-the-red-face, by whose hand mankind would know war, and Turongo-the-gentle who would lay down the foundations of peace. There was Haumia-the-abundant who was lord over the fruits of the earth and Ruaumoko-the-lastborn, whose one tiny movement would cause the earth herself to quake and tremor. Finally there was Tane-the-thoughtful, whose actions and deeds would produce the world and all its parts.

It was Tane who separated their parents to produce the sky above and the land below. And when his grieving parents' tears filled the world, he turned his mother over to stop Ranginui from having to look upon her face and be reminded of their separation.

Tane brought light to the world by placing the stars in the sky, the sun at its zenith and the moon lower down on his father's head. He built the first house of nobility and it remains to this day the blueprint from which all homes are templated. He filled it with the knowledge of the gods, which he retrieved from the summit of the heavens at the instruction of Io-the-creator himself. He produced the trees, the birds, the insects and fish to clothe and adorn his mother, the earth. Finally, he created the first human, a woman from whom all peoples are descended. The world of eternal light where all beings were kin, no matter who or what, was born.

Many times did summer and winter struggle in rivalry before Maui-of-the-topknot, half-man, half-god, was gifted to the world. Raised by his priestly elder, Tamanui, he was shown the secrets of the universe; the kinship that existed between all things that would allow him to take on the form of the tree, the bird, the fish, the lizard. He mastered himself and returned to his family ready to conquer.

With a fearless heart he secured the magic jawbone of knowledge of his ancestress Murirangawhenua. And with it he caught and slowed down the sun, which sped across the heavens at will with little thought for the activities of man. He made fire available to people by forcing the very last flame of the Keeper-of-the-fires, Mahuika, to become imbued into the heartwood of the tree. He visited the spirit world to find his father and before his death at the hands of the Goddess-of-death, Hine-nui-te-po, he fished up these sacred isles.

Using the sacred jawbone as a hook, Maui-the-relentless hauled up his great fish from the depths of Te Moananui a Kiwa, the Pacific Ocean. But as he paid homage to the gods for having given him such a wondrous gift, with greed in their eyes and lies on their tongues his four brothers took to the fish with knives. In its death throes it became torn and shredded with gullies and gorges, hills and mountains. In time, the stingray-like fish became the North Island of New Zealand while the canoe of Maui became the South Island.

The head of the fish is at our capital city, Wellington. The ridge of mountain ranges that run down the centre of the island is its backbone. To the east coast and west to Taranaki can be seen its fins. The stomach is Lake Taupo while the heart is at Maunga Pohatu in the Ureweras. Northland is the whipping tail of the stingray. From tip to tip, fish to canoe, can be seen the myriad of extremities of this once virgin land.

And many centuries ago, when the voyager Kupe with his family and wife came upon these islands shrouded in mist and cloud they named them Aotearoa, land of the long white cloud.

Chris Winitana

ALAN LEE

The rolling hill country of the Waikato provided the perfect location for Weathertop.

The landscapes of Middle-earth were forged in Tolkien's imagination from a combination of memories of places he'd known and the mythical lands he encountered during his studies of ancient texts. His descriptions of the *Shire*, the *Misty Mountains* and the golden woods of *Lothlórien* are evocative enough to make these places seem tangible, but we each bring our own memories and dreams into play when we imagine them. While his love of England may have been the foundation stone of Middle-earth, we didn't believe we would find there, or anywhere else in Europe, a landscape that was not so steeped in its own history that it could serve as the background for his epic. As a result, I found the prospect of looking for Middle-earth in a country reminiscent of Europe but lacking the accumulated and overlaid evidence of thousands of years of continual habitation intriguing.

We travelled widely to far-flung parts of the country, led by our location scout, Dave Comer, looking for the perfect *Hobbiton*, *Rivendell* and *Bree*, finding a lovely location for *Hobbiton*, with hills that looked as though Hobbits had already begun excavations. It had a lake with a long arm we could pass off as a river, the perfect spot for a bridge, a mill and '*The Green Dragon*', a *Party Tree* and an ideal situation for *Bag End*. It only needed an ancient tree, which our Greens Department, under Brian Massey, constructed and painstakingly foliated with plastic leaves. After several months of earth moving, set building, hedge laying and gardening the place

An incongruous combination. Light refreshments are undertaken on the 'slopes' of Caradhras.

PIERRE VINET

Mountain storms in the Wizard's Vale, near Glenorchy.

felt as though it had been inhabited by generations of Hobbits, and it was satisfying to see it had taken on something of the look of the Devonshire countryside I'd lived in for the past twenty-five years.

As we wanted a less benign and cultivated look for the countryside around *Bree* we ended up close to Wellington, where we used land owned by the military on the Miramar peninsula for the outskirts, while the *Prancing Pony* and surrounding streets were built around barracks at Fort Dorset, in Seatoun.

Mount Ruapehu was an obvious first stop in the search for *Mordor* and the site of the battle on the slopes of *Mount Doom*, with the prologue for *The Fellowship of the Ring* shot in the off-season ski field at Whakapapa. *Frodo* and *Sam* tramped back and forth over a nearby area Peter liked the look of for the *Emyn Muil* — the vast labyrinth of rocks our heroes have to find their way through on their journey to the *Black Gates*, and where they first meet *Gollum*.

The *Weathertop* scenes were shot on a station at Port Waikato, where strangely shaped limestone outcrops and disfigured trees in a green landscape wouldn't have been out of place in the background of an Hieronymus Bosch painting. We found the perfect hill for the *Ringwraiths*' attack, with the ruins of *Amon Sul* built in a studio and the wider views established in a matte painting.

Warriors from Harad prepare for battle at Twelve Mile Delta.

We visited Skippers Canyon several times looking for the ford where *Arwen* and *Frodo* face the *Ringwraiths*, and the digitally created flood you see in the finished movie was only slightly

ALAN LEE

PIERRE VINET

PIERRE VINET

PIERRE VINET

ALAN LEE

Opposite top: The Dead Marshes.

Opposite centre left: Peter Jackson and crew discuss angles at Paradise near Glenorchy.

Opposite centre right: Aragorn and Éowyn rehearse lines — Deer Park Heights.

Opposite bottom: Deer Park Heights near Queenstown provided a very useful location for filming. The Riders of Rohan stand tall above the civilisation below.

Above: The Dart River, Paradise.

more impressive than the real one that swept away one of our sets after a particularly heavy rainfall! I'm always looking for interesting rock formations and textures, which I use to ensure the 'bones' of any of my pictures also have a story to tell, and so that the rocks and stones I draw don't always look the same. Skippers Canyon provided some great material, and also formed a suitably grand setting for the Fellowship's journey down the *Anduin*, and for the *Argonath*.

Our search for *Rivendell* took us far and wide, but although we found useful elements, we never found one place with everything we wanted. We eventually chose Kaitoke because of its beautiful, calm woodlands and proximity to Wellington, but its surroundings in the film are a combination of filmed elements such as waterfalls, photographs, paintings and a miniature built at Weta Workshop, long before we knew where we would be filming.

Filming the Hobbits leaving the Shire on Mt Victoria.

PIERRE VINET

Paradise, near Glenorchy at the northern end of Lake Wakatipu, worked well for parts of *Lothlórien*, though we added larger trees, and for scenes at

Rivendell scene at Kaitoke Regional Park.

Parth Galen and *Amon Hen*. I loved the landscape around Poolburn, where many of the *Rohan* scenes were shot, with its rolling hills and dramatic granite tors reminding me of Dartmoor, although on a much grander scale. Mount Potts, near Methven, provided one of the most glorious locations, with an isolated hill in a wide valley, buttressed by sheer cliffs, which couldn't have been closer to Tolkien's *Edoras*. We built the exterior of the *Golden Hall* and surrounding buildings on top with the gatehouse and more buildings at its foot, with everything in between added post-production.

We were always on the lookout for wetland areas for the *Dead Marshes* between the *Emyn Muil* and the *Black Gates*. In the end all the scenes were shot on sets created by our Greens Department, with wider views shot from helicopters. Once we'd landed, we quickly realised the impracticality of filming in a place where we'd have to count the crew after each take.

I found New Zealand more than matched my hopes as a setting for *The Lord of the Rings*. It has such a wide variety of landscapes, from lush farmland, woods and rivers to dramatic gorges, endless plains and soaring mountains uninterrupted by roads and pylons. It's a young land, primeval in places, still flexing in the aftermath of its creation. I can imagine Britain in a much earlier age, with higher peaks and the clearer light that illuminates Tolkien's pages, might have had a similar quality.

It has been a pleasure, and a privilege, to have seen so much of New Zealand's rich and beautiful landscapes with guides whose wealth of experience was matched only by their love of their country and enthusiasm for our journey.

Alan Lee
Conceptual Artist/Set Decorator

Hobbiton

PIERRE VINET

The Waikato region of the North Island is one of the richest farming areas in New Zealand. Driving south on State Highway One, the urban sprawl of Auckland is soon replaced by paddocks and hedgerows.

A district of rolling grassy hills, Matamata is a small part of England transported to the other side of the world. The name means point or headland in Maori, and the area was named after Te Waharoa Pa, which jutted out into a swamp, rendering it impregnable.

The area's development can be accredited to an Englishman, Josiah Clifton Firth, who emigrated from Yorkshire in 1855. Travelling south on business, he established a lasting friendship with local Maori and by 1884 had purchased 56,000 acres of swampy marshland. With a strong vision for the area, he commenced large-scale drainage of the fens and planted vast paddocks in grass, barley, wheat and oats. In the ensuing years the area was transformed as hedgerows grew alongside oaks and elms and the area prospered as the railway probed south from Auckland. Today Matamata remains a country service town, with the cheese factory Firth developed at Waharoa still turning milk from local farms into cheese. Matamata's rich grassland now produces

Above: Sam Gamgee and Frodo leaving the Shire.

Below: A signpost in Matamata town centre.

Welcome to
Hobbiton

IAN BRODIE

INTERNET	INTERNET
www.waikatonz.co.nz	www.hobbiton.info.

Above: Hobbiton in the peaceful Shire.

Below: Gandalf the Grey greets Bilbo at Bag End

another lucrative crop; the Waikato has developed into New Zealand's main racehorse-breeding area.

There are two routes to this town of wide streets and friendly faces — turn off before Pokeno and travel on SH27, or continue on SH1 through Hamilton and turn left towards Piarere.

Venture south of Matamata on Hinuera Road (SH27) and it soon becomes apparent why Hobbiton was created here, thousands of kilometres from Sarehole and Tolkien's rural England; the hedgerow-lined lanes provide glimpses of paddocks and grassy downs that are a vision of the *Shire*.

Pause at Piarere — the strange rock formations reveal this whole valley was once a riverbed, with rocky escarpments left stranded high on the sides of hills that once channelled water. Known as the Hinuera Formation, these rocks are a set of alluvial sands, gravels and silts deposited in the basin during the period of the Last Glaciation (between 50,000 and 15,000 years ago). In 1999, these paddocks were transformed into the Green Hill Country of the *Shire, Middle-earth*.

Amble down Puketutu Road and turn onto the appropriately named Buckland Road. Bordered by hawthorn, the road winds through a valley before climbing to a lookout providing a perfect vantage point for the distant Kaimai Ranges.

Returning to town, the Workman's Café in the

ALAN LEE

main street is a local icon. With its eccentric décor and slightly eccentric staff, it makes a welcome stop for lunch or dinner.

A drive on Tower Road allows a visit to the original home of Josiah Firth before continuing to Wairere Falls, set amongst the beautiful bush of the Kaimai Ranges. Dropping over the Okauia Fault in two stages of 80 and 73 metres, the falls are a 45-minute walk on a track that closely follows the boulder-strewn Wairere Stream. En route is a viewpoint of the Matamata Plains, and on clearer days the mountains of Tongariro National Park to the south.

The drive back to town provides another distraction, the Opal Hot Springs, where you can soak away the grime of a day's travel.

Anyone with an interest in thoroughbred horses should take an early drive to the local racecourse and see over 500 horses being taken for their morning exercise as the sun rises over the horizon.

IAN BRODIE

Above top: Bagshot Row, as seen in *The Fellowship of the Ring.*

Above: Hobbit holes around The Hill.

Below: Bag End today.

IAN BRODIE

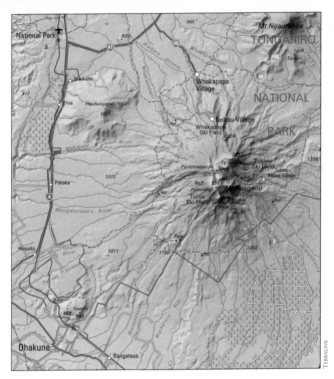

Above: The Tongariro National Park and its environs.

Right: Iwikau Village, a key part of Mordor.

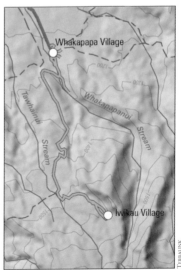

The Central North Island is an area of distinctive geography and contrasting scenery. In the space of an hour you can travel from a peaceful wonderland of rivers, lakes and pastoral greenery to a blasted, tormented landscape of lava and volcanic ash.

This area was once one of the most prolific volcanic areas in the world, with Lake Taupo formed as a result of the largest eruption seen in the last 5000 years. The Oruanui Eruption, 26,500 years ago, created the shape of the lake, then in 181 AD a further explosion produced an eruption column 50 km high with over 30 km of pumice, ash and rock fragments ejected in minutes. The effects of the eruption were seen in the sky as far away as Europe and China.

Sitting beside New Zealand's largest lake (619 km²) Taupo serves as an ideal base for visiting all areas of the volcanic plateau, including the thermal resort of Rotorua, the world-famous fishing area of the Tongariro River or the mountainous region of Tongariro National Park.

Home to a kaleidoscope of bubbling mud, geysers and pristine lakes, the thermal wonderland of Rotorua is a one-hour drive to the north and one of the most popular tourist destinations in New Zealand.

South of Taupo is Tongariro National Park, New Zealand's first national park and a world heritage area. The park was created in 1887 when three volcanoes, Ruapehu, Ngauruhoe and Tongariro, were gifted to the people of New Zealand by Ngati Tuwharetoa, the local iwi.

Above: Lake Taupo, a boatie's paradise.

Below: Lake Taupo.

New Zealand is gorgeous! I don't really think that there's anywhere else we could have filmed this movie unless we had travelled to lots of different places around the world. Every element of Middle-earth is contained in New Zealand. It's perfect. There are so many different geographical landscapes: mountains, woods, marshes, desert areas, rolling hills — and the sea. Everything, in fact, described in The Lord of the Rings.

Elijah Wood

INTERNET

www.laketauponz.co.nz

VIGGO MORTENSEN

Above: Tawhai Falls near the Grand Chateau.

Below: The Noldorin elf Gil-galad wielding the mighty spear Aeglos.

IAN BRODIE

The drive from Taupo to the Grand Chateau follows SH1 around Lake Taupo to Turangi, a good stop for anglers wishing to fish the world-famous Tongariro River. A licence, obtained from information centres and local Department of Conservation (DOC) offices, is required to fish New Zealand lakes, and it would be wise to check on the local fishing season.

At Rangipo turn right onto SH46 and after 41 km turn left onto SH48 — the Grand Chateau is a further 10 km on. Pause at Tawhai Falls, 4 km up this road and take the twenty-minute walk which will give you a view of the falls, which are well worth a visit. The beech and toatoa-lined river tumbling over an ancient lava flow into a rock pool can easily be imagined as *Henneth Annûn*.

The Grand Chateau, one of the most iconic hotels in New Zealand, sits in splendid isolation at the foot of Mt Ruapehu in Tongariro National Park. Just one hour's drive south from Taupo, the hotel was built in the 1920s and features huge floor to ceiling windows to make the most of the outstanding views.

The *Lord of the Rings* team stayed here for a number of weeks, using the conference room as their headquarters and the cinema to view the film 'rushes'. The great advantage of staying at this hotel, of course, is the ability to drive 15 minutes and be transported into the heart of *Mordor*.

The highest peak in the North Island, Mt Ruapehu (2796 m) has an explosive history, with eruptions last century spreading ash as far south as Wellington. The simmering crater is strongly acidic and occasionally mud and rock are thrown down the mountainside. Part of a volcanic chain extending as far as Tonga, extensive seismic measuring equipment ensures ample warning is received of any impending explosion.

PIERRE VINET

INTERNET	**INTERNET**
www.chateau.co.nz	www.ruapehu.tourism.co.nz

PIERRE VINET

Orcs gather to attack at the Battle of the Last Alliance.

In winter, Whakapapa Ski Field is a playground for skiers who enjoy the après-ski lifestyle. In other seasons it is transformed into an area of mountainous volcanic rock.

To visit the area used to portray the battle marking the end of the Second Age of Middle-earth, drive to Iwikau Village, fifteen minutes up the slope from the Grand Chateau. The location is easily accessible but stout walking shoes are recommended. With blasted volcanic rock, steep bluffs and ash, little imagination is required to envisage *Mordor*.

From the main building head north around the learners' ski slope towards Pinnacle Ridge. Before climbing this, walk slightly downhill and along the ridge to a viewpoint of a tumbled area with steep escarpments. As it's hard to be specific about this location, the GPS coordinates are the only precise direction. The slopes and nearby car park saw Orcs attacking Elves and Men, with *Elrond* standing fast. The special-effects team at Weta Studios then added thousands of other 'actors' to complete the scene.

Special care was undertaken during filming in all sensitive ecological areas and many acres of carpet were laid out for the Orcs and Elves to walk on, protecting the ground underneath.

> *The Great Battle of the Last Alliance was an effort by Elves and Men to rid the world of Sauron's great evil. The second largest army to muster in Middle-earth met a huge Orc host upon Dagorlad Plain in 3431 (SA). Sauron retreated to Barad-dûr and for seven years the alliance laid siege. In the year 3441(SA) he emerged to do battle and in the conflict the Elven king Gil-galad was destroyed but Isildur managed to cut the ring from Sauron's finger before perishing.*

VIEWPOINT OF ROCK WHERE ISILDUR CUT THE RING FROM SAURON: S39° 14.116—E175° 33.529

ROCK WALL LOCATION OF ABOVE: S39° 14.114—E175° 33.522

Tongariro Crossing
Plains of Gorgoroth

DESTINATION LAKE TAUPO

Above: Mt Ruapehu wears a mantle of snow.

Below: The Tongariro Crossing walk.

Opposite top: Mangawhero Falls.

Opposite bottom: Rangers of Ithilien in their distinctive camouflaged clothing.

To really feel the isolation of this area and to immerse oneself in *Mordor*, the Tongariro Crossing is a highly recommended and very popular day tramp. Passing over a varied and spectacular terrain in the presence of two active volcanoes, the tramp passes a cold mountain spring, lava flows, an active crater, emerald coloured lakes and hot springs.

The tramp does need to be treated seriously as it crosses open and exposed alpine terrain, often subject to severe weather conditions. The local DOC office at the Chateau will provide more detailed information.

Taking 7–8 hours, the tramp commences at Mangatepopo (6 km off SH47) and terminates at Ketetahi, and suitable transportation is required to return to the starting point. A number of transport companies operate shuttle services.

DESTINATION LAKE TAUPO

Ithilien Camp

To reach the next location, take a short drive to the village of Ohakune, where the rich volcanic soil lays claim to the largest production area of carrots in New Zealand. Unless skiing is on your agenda, winter isn't the best time to visit. During the colder months the town bustles as the many bars and restaurants swell with skiers reliving the day's runs and spills on the slopes. The 'O' Bar staff remember the filming in this locality very well; the establishment was the scene of a serious party, held to celebrate its completion.

To reach the general area of filming for the *Ithilien Camp* travel up the Turoa Ski Field road (also known as the Ohakune Mountain Road Scenic Drive). After much fundraising and work by volunteers, the Ohakune Mountain Road opened in 1963. There are a number of walks and tramps off this road (again visit the local DOC Centre for more information).

The hidden outpost of Henneth Annûn (Sindarin 'Window of the Sunset') was constructed by Gondor as a strategic base from which to undertake guerrilla operations against the Harad and Orcs of Sauron. Accessed by a secret passage from the forest it consisted of a number of caves hidden by a high waterfall and was used in later years by the Rangers of Ithilien as both a refuge and base.

The exact filming site is not publicly accessible but travel up the road through the beautiful mountain beech as far as the Mangawhero Falls. Some of the filming of the *Ithilien Camp* was undertaken in the nearby bush. The falls themselves are reminiscent of *Hennuth Annûn* so it becomes a pleasant drive. The road climbs steadily, providing great views of Mt Ruapehu in one direction and the rolling hills around Ohakune in the other.

IAN BRODIE

The *River Anduin* is an hour's drive away via Waiouru and then south on SH1 to Taihape. The National Army Museum at Waiouru makes a worthwhile visit — a number of well-presented displays portray the story of New Zealand's land-based forces in both peace and wartime.

PIERRE VINET

RANGITIKEI RIVER RAFTING

IAN BRODIE

Above: A Rangitikei River Raft floats gently down the Anduin.

Below: View from the bridge at Hightime Bungy.

Opposite top: Frodo and Sam in the forests of Ithilien.

Opposite bottom: Waitarere Forest tracks are suitable for mountain bikes.

The *River Anduin* in the *Fellowship of the Ring* incorporated four different New Zealand rivers, the Rangitikei River near Taihape appearing first. A young river in geological terms, the Rangitikei has carved sheer cliff walls on its way to the Tasman Sea.

The quickest way to approach the location is to drive a little way south from Taihape and turn left at Ohutu. A bungy jump (the highest in the North Island) is situated near the location so follow the 'Hightime Bungy' signs for approximately 15 minutes on a charming scenic drive through bush with scenes of 'heartland' New Zealand. After reaching the bungy site park your car and walk across the one-way traffic bridge. An amazing scene is revealed, as the unspoiled river appears 80 m below, flowing through a gorge of enormous proportions.

The Moawhango River, at its confluence with the Rangitikei, was also used to portray the *Anduin* and as you return to the main road cross via the next one-way bridge. Park at the far end and walk back onto it for another scene of a steep fern-lined gorge with the Moawhango rushing towards the Rangitikei.

To make your own trip down the *Anduin* drive south 18 km to Mangaweka. Beneath the distinctive DC-3 café is the headquarters of Rangitikei River Rafting. River safety specialists for the filming in this area, they offer a full day eco-tour entitled 'Grand Canyons of the Rangitikei' past the exact site. Suitable for all ages, their oar-powered rafts mean you can sit back and enjoy the scenery as you drift quietly downstream. Your tour will also reveal the wonders of concretionary boulders and ancient shellfish of a past era.

INTERNET	BRIDGE OVER RIVER ANDUIN
www.riveradventures.net.nz	S39° 42.279—E175° 58.238

Trollshaw Forest and Osgiliath Wood

Pierre Vinet

Ian Brodie

Waitarere Forest is located south of Foxton on the Kapiti Coast. From the north, after passing Poroutawhao watch for the turning to Waitarere Beach on your right. The Kapiti Coast is a popular summer holiday area for many Wellingtonians who come to relax at the many beaches along the coast. Waitarere Beach is a typical beach village with the ever-present camping grounds and ice-cream parlours.

Just as you enter Waitarere a small unnamed side road on the right allows entry to a parking area on the edge of the forest. Vehicle access is not permitted any further, which provides good justification for a walk on any of a number of well-formed tracks under the tall trees.

The plantation forest stretches for some kilometres both north and south of Waitarere and is very different to native bush, with most of the trails also suitable for mountain bikes.

Filming was undertaken in a number of different parts of the park, including *Osgiliath Wood*, *Trollshaw Forest* and scenes of *Arwen* riding through the trees.

Situated west of Rivendell, the Trollshaw Forest was the haunt of Trolls who travelled down from the Ettenmoors. In the year 2941 (TA) Bilbo Baggins was captured by three trolls but managed to keep them arguing until the sun rose and they turned to stone.

INTERNET

www.rivernz.com

IAN BRODIE

Above: The dense bush of the Otaki Gorge Road.

Below: Gandalf the Grey leading the Hobbits away from the Shire.

Opposite top: The end of the Otaki Gorge Road.

Opposite bottom: Gandalf prepares to depart the Shire for Minas Tirith.

The town of Otaki, a one-hour drive north of Wellington, is rich in both sunshine and history. Maori settlement of the area was as early as the 1300s and the small village continued its peaceful existence until 1819, when the Ngati Toa invasion (under the famous chief Te Rauparaha) culminated in the Battle of Waiorua in 1826. With Te Rauparaha established as paramount chief there was constant inter-tribal fighting but in 1839 the missionary Octavius Hadfield arrived from the Bay of Islands, in an attempt to restore peace through 'Christianisation'.

By 1886 the railway had reached the expanding village bringing an influx of settlers to mill timber, clear land and continue to extend the railway. Farming developed in the ensuing years and in the late 1930s a number of market gardeners moved north to produce the ever-increasing quantities of fruit and vegetables required for the city markets.

Today Otaki is almost a dormitory city of Wellington, with commuters making the hour-long trip to Wellington each day, although market gardening and farming are still major industries.

The nearby Otaki Gorge Road was used to portray the young Hobbits' journey to the border of their beloved *Shire* through peaceful and productive gardens and farms, providing an interesting parallel with Otaki's real-life industries.

The turn-off to the Otaki Gorge is on the left just south of Otaki after crossing the Otaki River. Initially sealed, it soon becomes a narrow unpaved road so care should be taken over the 19-km journey, especially for drivers who are not used to driving in these conditions.

PIERRE VINET

INTERNET

www.centrestage.co.nz

Although the specific locations used to show the Hobbits leaving the *Shire* in *The Fellowship of the Ring* are not accessible to the public, the trip to the Otaki Gorge is highly recommended. The transformation of scenery during the short drive up the gorge is quite remarkable, and provides a useful insight into exactly why New Zealand proved to be the perfect place to film *The Lord of the Rings* trilogy. Leaving the rolling farm country behind, the road soon narrows and plunges into beautiful rimu and rata bush. Breaks in the bush on the side of the road reveal glimpses of the Otaki River as it flows through the gorge on its way to the Tasman Sea.

IAN BRODIE

The scenery here is very reminiscent of Tolkien's description of the outer reaches of the *Shire* and once the end of the road is reached there are a number of excellent picnic spots beside the river, with the bush providing cool and welcome relief from the hot summer sun.

In another interesting parallel, a four-day tramp is also available from this end of the road, climbing across the Ruahine Range to the Kaitoke Regional Park (see page 38) in Upper Hutt, parts of which were used to portray *Rivendell*.

New Zealand is the ideal place to shoot these films. The land mass is so young, so savage, so untamed and unruly, all of which make it special.

Cate Blanchett

PIERRE VINET

Above: Wellington Harbour.

Below: Downtown Wellington.

Opposite: Te Papa Tongarewa.

To any enthusiast of *The Lord of the Rings* films, Wellington is Production Central, home to Peter Jackson, 3 Foot 6, Wingnut Films, Weta Workshop and Weta Digital. As Peter Jackson has said: 'I feel incredibly proud that this country, and especially this town, is responsible for what we have done.'

Bookshops promote Tolkien in their front window, Orcs produced by Sideshow Weta stare back from specialty-shop windows and there's even a Minister of Middle-earth.

Wellington nestles between a magnificent harbour and forest-clad hills, creating a compact downtown area with an intimacy uncommon in many other cities.

The earliest name for Wellington is Te Upoko o te ika a Maui, which means the head of Maui's fish. The Polynesian explorer, Kupe, is credited with the initial discovery of Wellington Harbour around the tenth century. The first European settlement was named Wellington after the first Duke of Wellington, by the directors of the New Zealand Company, whose first vessel arrived in 1839.

In November 1863 a resolution was moved by Parliament, then situated in Auckland, that a more central site was needed for the capital and the first sitting was held in Wellington on 26 July 1865.

Fire and earthquakes have since destroyed many early buildings but for those with an interest in early architecture the Nairn Street Cottage (68 Nairn Street) is a survivor from 1858. Also worthy of a visit is the Government Building on Lambton Quay; designed to look like stone, it is constructed entirely of wood. Nearby Parliament House and the Beehive should be included in any itinerary with daily tours available.

INTERNET

www.wellingtonNZ.com

Downtown sites

TOTALLY WELLINGTON

The centre of downtown Wellington is very easy to negotiate so put on some walking shoes and spend a day visiting some famous and interesting sights. A good place to start is the Museum of New Zealand, Te Papa Tongarewa, on Cable Street. Receiving worldwide acclaim for its exciting modern approach, the museum features a number of 'hands-on' exhibitions. Admission is free but charges apply to some exhibitions.

On the corner of Jervois Quay and Cable Street is The Film Centre, New Zealand's Museum of the Moving Image, and well worth a look. Admission is free. Nearby at 10 Kent Terrace is the Embassy, Wellington's grandest cinema, venue for the Australasian premiere of *The Fellowship of the Ring*. Host again for the release of *The Two Towers* in December 2002, the Embassy has recently been totally refurbished and features many refinements, which have seen the grand old theatre restored to its former glory. Boasting the largest screen in the country and superb digital sound, watching a movie at the Embassy is an experience not to be missed.

For those wishing a more permanent souvenir of 'Wellywood' walk around to Dymocks Booksellers at 360 Lambton Quay. They have the largest range of Tolkien books in New Zealand and stock the Sideshow Weta collectible figures.

In December 2001 the red carpet was rolled out and Ringwraiths rode on horseback when the Embassy Cinema hosted the Australasian premiere of The Fellowship of the Ring. To quote Elijah Wood, 'They said it was going to be massive and suddenly I felt like a rock star . . . '

A more unusual location is the WestpacTrust Stadium on the waterfront. During the lunch break in a one-day cricket match between New Zealand and England, Peter Jackson extolled the crowd of 30,000 to stamp and chant in the Black Speech. The sounds were used for the Orcs' chants during the Battle of Helm's Deep.

PIERRE VINET

Above: The green tunnel leads to a frightening encounter for the Hobbits.

Below: The ridge on Mt Victoria used to film the race to the ferry.

Opposite top: The Hobbits take refuge from the Nazgûl as they flee the Shire.

Opposite bottom: The location for a perfect Hobbit-hiding place.

While on paper the centre of a metropolitan area may seem to be an unlikely location for the rural *Shire*, Mt Victoria's role in *The Fellowship of the Ring* movie is a direct result of the foresight of Wellington's town planners. With a superb view from the summit — stretching from Cook Strait in the south to the city of Wellington in the north — Mt Victoria is part of an encircling green belt. Its forests and landscape provided the perfect location for the *Outer Shire*, along with easy accessibility for the cast and crew, something that was not always easy to achieve. It also marked the commencement of shooting on 11 October 1999, and the beginning of a 274-day journey that would take the cast and crew throughout the country.

The easiest way to reach the locations is to drive along Alexandra Road, which will eventually take you to the summit. The road has a number of parking areas, so watch for one on your left about halfway up in the apex of a sweeping right-hand turn. The track on your left plunges downhill through a forest and after another right-hand turn the view ahead is instantly recognisable.

Like a green tunnel the straight path leads through two banks with dark overhanging trees, and no

IAN BRODIE

LOCATION OF PATH
S 41° 18.101—E 174° 47.293

imagination is required to picture *Frodo* standing in the middle of the path, listening fearfully for the approaching *Nazgûl*. The city below is invisible, the area one of quiet solitude with rustling trees and chirping insects completing this scene of a rural path in the *Shire*.

Continue down the same path and as it turns to the right two further locations unfold. The steep bank on your left marks the spot where the Hobbits slid down to discover a feast of mushrooms.

On your right up the hill are two trees with a small overhanging ledge. Here a large manufactured tree was transplanted to provide a more realistic root system for the Hobbits to hide under. It was here the frightened Hobbits hid to escape the *Nazgûl*, with the worms and spiders escaping from the ground in revulsion at his evilness.

The path winds down through the woods towards the city and on a warm summer's day, the scent of pine needles and the tall trees standing against a blue sky create an idyllic and surprisingly peaceful spot.

Unit Publicist Claire Raskind-Cooper recalls how the press had discovered this area was to be used for the first day of filming. 'I remember running up the bank asking the photographers to move back.'

There are parts that are really like Scotland — only bigger! Maybe it's Scotland as seen by a Hobbit!

Billy Boyd

LOCATION OF TREE HOBBITS HID UNDER: S 41° 18.075—E 174° 47.319

(NB THESE COORDINATES ARE FROM THE PATH)

IAN BRODIE

View from the summit of the Rimutaka Ranges road.

The Wairarapa covers a wide area with a diverse range of spectacular landscapes. Situated an hour north of Wellington, it's a popular escape with vineyards, adventure activities and tourist trails. The vineyards also became a popular haunt for the *Lord of the Rings* cast.

Driving north on SH2 the urban areas of the Hutt Valley are soon replaced by bush-covered hills as the road climbs over the Rimutaka Ranges. A spectacular route, the road ascends through a number of valleys before reaching the summit, with fabulous views of Featherston and the Wairarapa.

The Rimutaka Ranges proved a major obstacle until the railway arrived in Featherston in 1878. This was no ordinary train track, and the steepness of the climb required a friction-drive system. Designed by John Fell, the Fell Engine featured smooth horizontal powered wheels held against a raised centre-rail that pulled the train up the Incline. Operating from 1878 to 1955, the high cost of operations necessitated the construction of a tunnel through the ranges. The 8.798 km tunnel opened on

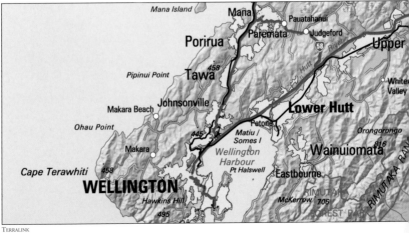

TERRALINK

IAN BRODIE

29 October 1955 and the dutiful little Fell Engines were cut up for scrap. Only one survived, now on display in the Fell Museum at Featherston, and beautifully restored to her former glory.

Featherston has grown considerably since the opening of the Rimutaka Tunnel and residents now travel to work in the Hutt Valley and Wellington.

Featherston is also host to Fernside, one of New Zealand's finest historic homes. To stay in this magnificent residence is a tonic in itself, but the other reason for a stay here is to wander the gardens of *Lothlórien*.

Lothlórien, realm of Celeborn and Galadriel.

INTERNET

www.wairarapanz.com

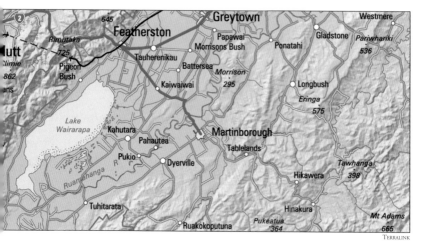

TERRALINK

Lothlórien and the Gladden Fields

PIERRE VINET

Lothlórien (Sindarin 'Dream-flower') had been the dwelling of the high Elven queen Galadriel, the Lady of Lórien, for thousands of years. Situated beside the River Celebrant west of the Anduin, the realm of Galadriel and Celeborn was home to the gold and silver mellyrn trees. The Elves dwelt in the boughs upon platforms (talan) and were also called the Galadhrim, or tree people.

Fernside provides an opportunity to drift back to the peace and tranquillity of a bygone era. Created by Ella and Charles Elgar in 1924 to satisfy Mrs Elgar's wish to entertain the rich and influential, Fernside is a gracious home with large rooms including a library, dining and drawing rooms. Accommodation is available in one of four original en-suite bedrooms and rooms are also available for private functions.

The gardens are an absolute delight and it's no wonder they were chosen to portray *Lothlórien*. In the style of English garden designer Gertrude Jekyll, they feature a number of 'garden rooms' with their own distinctive plantings. The man-made lake was used to portray the departure from *Lothlórien* as well as scenes depicting *Sméagol* and *Déagol* fishing near the *Gladden Fields*, which were not included in the theatrical release.

Although not filmed, the wooded walks are beautiful, especially in the autumn. To walk under the golden trees with fallen leaves underfoot is an absolute delight.

Note: this site is *not* open to the public. These locations are only accessible by staying in the house. Refer to the website for further information.

INTERNET
www.fernside.co.nz

PIERRE VINET

The diversity of landscape in the Upper Hutt region made it ideal for filming for a number of reasons.

The proximity of nearby studios minimised Peter Jackson's logistical problems of flying hundreds of people to other parts of the country, often for only a short scene.

The town of Upper Hutt is a pleasant 40-minute drive through the Hutt Valley from Wellington and makes an ideal base from which to explore the region. Away from cosmopolitan Wellington, Upper Hutt has a smaller village feel, with all the facilities one would expect to find in a major city.

The Hutt Valley has been continuosly occupied for over 800 years and when the people of Te Ati Awa arrived they used the river as both a source of plentiful food and an efficient transport route, naming it Te Awa Kairangi, or 'highly esteemed river'.

European settlers arrived in the region in 1839 but the Valley grew slowly, mainly due to the swampy nature of the land. This all changed dramatically when a major earthquake in 1855 raised the level of the Hutt Valley and drained the surrounding wetland, making it suitable for farming.

Today, the city of Upper Hutt occupies a large area and its numerous parks, native bush reserves and river combine with easy access to make it a very pleasant suburban city. There are a number of indoor and outdoor attractions in the area as well as a superb boutique cinema called The Lighthouse. It's almost like watching movies at home; seating fewer than 30 people it features a large screen and excellent sound.

TOTALLY WELLINGTON

Opposite top: Sméagol and Déagol fishing near the Gladden Fields.

Opposite bottom: The Celebrant flows through Lothlórien.

Above: The Hutt River.

Below: Kaitoke Regional Park.

IAN BRODIE

INTERNET

www.uhcc.govt.nz

Rivendell and the Fords of Isen

IAN BRODIE

IAN BRODIE

Kaitoke Regional Park nestles in the foothills of the Tararua Ranges, 12 km north of Upper Hutt. The park contains some 2800 hectares of mature native forest and is popular for picnics, swimming and walking with the more than 100,000 visitors who visit annually.

To enter the park turn off SH2 and travel down Waterworks Road to the Pakuratahi – Hutt Forks car park. Four walks begin near here and there are many pleasant picnic spots along the rivers and bush fringes. Camping is available on the grassy flats at Kaitoke where toilets and coin-operated barbecues are also available. The clear pools on the Hutt and Pakuratahi Rivers are ideal for swimming.

The position of Rivendell is signposted from the entrance to the park and at the location itself there is an interpretative display showing the construction and final result. Although most exterior shots were digitally rendered, the set constructors built a large set at Kaitoke, including the bedroom where *Frodo* recovered from his knife attack. The impressive site included scaffolding out into the river itself along with a man-made river and waterfalls to suit the filmmakers' requirements. Over 30 workers began construction in November 1999 and the set was completed in March 2000, with filming undertaken between April and May 2000. During actual filming there were more than 300 crew on site. The temperate rainforest and river made this beautiful area an ideal representation of *Rivendell*.

Looking down over the bridge by the car park the *Fords of Isen* and the spot where *Éomer* finds the wounded *Théodred* can be seen.

Rivendell was a translation of the Sindarin name Imladris (deep cloven valley) and was situated in the foothills of the western Misty Mountains. Elrond founded this refuge in the wilderness (the Last Homely House East of the Sea) in 1797 (SA) after retreating from the evil of Sauron.

INTERNET:	RIVENDELL SITE: S 41° 03.438—E 175° 11.666
www.wrc.govt.nz	DRESSING ROOMS ETC: S 41° 03.446—E 174° 11.617

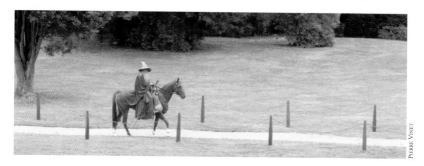

PIERRE VINET

To travel from *Rivendell* to *Isengard* was an arduous journey of many weeks with countless leagues of wild rough country to negotiate but in Upper Hutt it can be completed in less than 15 minutes. A pleasant oasis in suburbia, Harcourt Park was utilised for three different *Isengard* scenes and is situated on Akatarawa Road; a right turn off SH2 if returning from Kaitoke. There is accommodation available right next door at the Harcourt Holiday Park.

An elevated section of the park was transformed into the gardens of *Isengard* where *Gandalf* and *Saruman* first met after the rediscovery of the ring at *Hobbiton*. It is located across a green lawn and up a small rise with a park-bench situated at the top. Looking down from the garden you can see another two sites, although virtually nothing now remains to mark the spot. At the time of writing a slightly discernable track (mainly noticeable by the change in grass colour) could be seen running through the middle of the lawn. During filming, the lawn was removed and a gravel pathway formed complete with a chain-link fence on each side. Sound familiar? It was the entrance road into *Isengard*. Once the scenes were completed it was totally removed and the lawn replanted, a tribute to the care and attention of *The Lord of the Rings* crew.

Opposite top: Area set aside for dressing rooms, Kaitoke Regional Park.

Opposite bottom: Luxuriant foliage — Rivendell.

Above: Gandalf the Grey arrives at Isengard.

Below: Gandalf the Grey and Saruman the White in the gardens of Isengard.

PIERRE VINET

ISENGARD GARDENS
S 41° 06.069—E 175° 05.644

CHRIS COAD

Above: Saruman's Orcs wasted no time in felling the beautiful trees of Isengard.

Below: The same scene today is certainly less terrifying.

Harcourt Park is also home to the famous hinged trees of *Isengard*. During the transformation of *Saruman*'s lair a number of trees needed to be filmed being cut down to provide fuel for his furnaces.

These scenes would need to be filmed a number of times and the set designers took a novel approach. First of all, two trees were cut down from a remote location and transported (roots and all) over 200 km, with each section of cut branch numbered to enable re-assembly.

Two holes were dug and iron poles driven into the ground, and the trees reassembled by bolting all the branches together before they were 'planted' attached to the iron poles and effectively hinged. This meant they could be 'cut' down, brought back up and 'cut' down again while being filmed from a different angle. As the trees didn't have enough leaves, a team spent two weeks wiring on plastic ones.

The results were spectacular. Filmed in the rain, the trees toppled on command (after a few teething troubles) and after a week of filming some spectacular footage was obtained and mixed digitally to portray the infamous makeover of *Isengard*. The trees have since been removed.

Unrelated to *The Lord of the Rings*, this park is also home to one of the best examples of an earthquake fault line in New Zealand. The Wellington Fault passes through the park and in the nineteenth century a large earthquake shook this area, lifting the ground some 5 m and diverting the course of the Hutt River. The fault, which is signposted within the park and visited regularly by geology students, is well worth a visit.

IAN BRODIE

SMALLER HINGED TREE:	S 41° 06.109—E 175° 05.612
LARGER HINGED TREE:	S 41° 06.109—E 175° 05.624

River Anduin

The Hutt River flows for some 30 km from its source in the Southern Tararua Ranges through bush, farmland and city before finally entering the sea at Petone. Activity along the Wellington Fault over the last 2 million years has caused the formation of the river, shattering and weakening the underlying bedrock and forming the associated floodplain. The river was an important transport link for both Maori and European settlers and a foot track followed its banks for many kilometres before continuing over the Rimutaka Hill to the Wairarapa. Despite its proximity to suburbia, remnants of the original vegetation remain on its banks in many places and its natural beauty provided an ideal site for filming the River Anduin, close to the Wellington studios.

IAN BRODIE

Above: A comparison photo of the Hutt River (see below).

Below: The Fellowship used small Elven boats to travel down the Anduin to Amon Hen.

Principal filming was undertaken on the river between Moonshine and Totara Park although further smaller scenes were shot at Kaitoke in the north. The river can be accessed off SH2. After crossing the Moonshine Bridge (heading north) watch for the access road on your left just past Poet's Park. The small Elven boats were launched into the river here many times, with a number of close shots of the travellers originating from this locality.

Another great way to follow the river is to walk all or part of the Hutt River Trail starting at Petone in the south and ending 24 km later in Upper Hutt. For those without time to walk the entire track there's an access point at the Moonshine Bridge enabling a short stroll along the bank to Totara Park. It makes a pleasant diversion — civilisation seems very far away.

PIERRE VINET

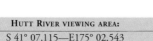

HUTT RIVER VIEWING AREA:
S 41° 07.115—E175° 02.543

PIERRE VINET

Above: A detail of Elvish architecture at Rivendell.

Below: Saruman the White, before his downfall into evil.

A day tour of the locations in and around Wellington is easily achieved and will allow you to see a diverse range of geography as well as some of the most easily recognisable scenes. Grab a map, make an early start and drive initially to Kent Terrace for a look at the Embassy Theatre — location of the Australasian Premiere of *The Fellowship of the Ring* and *The Two Towers.* Continue on to Pirie Street, park your car just prior to entering the bus tunnel, and venture into the wooded Mt Victoria town belt for a wander around the outskirts of the *Shire* and the *Race to the Ferry.*

To maintain your sustenance and savour the tastiest brunch in town, head to the Chocolate Fish Café. Once you're suitably replenished return to Wellington City and drive out on the motorway (SH2) to Kaitoke Regional Park and the location of *Rivendell.*

Down the road is Harcourt Park in Upper Hutt, which became the *Gardens of Isengard* in 2000. Trees, gardens and picnic spots abound as well as the location of the famous 'hinged' trees of *Isengard.*

The nearby Hutt River from Moonshine Bridge to Poet's Park was used for close-up filming of the Fellowship on the *River Anduin* and is ideal for a short stroll before returning to Wellington. If time permits, pause at Dry Creek Quarry at the bottom of Haywards Hill to see the set for *Helm's Deep.*

Dinner at the Arizona Bar & Grill should replenish even the most famished before returning to the Embassy Theatre to catch one of your favourite films, the ideal end to a day of adventure and discovery. Wellington hosts an excellent public transportation system and all of these locations are accessible by bus or train, although you would need to allow more time than if travelling by car.

PIERRE VINET

cafés and entertainment

Based in Wellington for an extended period, the cast found plenty of opportunities to let off steam.

It's easy to see why one of the most popular locations for the crew was the Chocolate Fish Café, situated at Scorching Bay. Close to Seatoun where the cast lived during filming, it provides excellent food and good service with a little eccentricity — the

IAN BRODIE

Above: Prime seating at the Chocolate Fish Café.

Below: At night, Wellington comes alive.

Chocolate Fish must be one of the few restaurants in the world with a main street running through its centre. Occupying a small house, tables are available both inside and out but the best seating is on the other side of the road, right beside the sea. Wearing bright day-glo vests, staff cross the road to deliver food and coffee to their guests 'on the other side'.

Downtown, the Arizona Bar & Grill, on the corner of Grey and Featherston Streets, brings a little of the southwest to town. Open seven days for lunch and dinner, the bar is a very popular spot with office workers on a Friday night. Fancy a free drink? During certain hours (after each purchase) the barman spins a wheel of fortune with the opportunity of winning a free round or free fries.

Other favourite nightspots of Liv Tyler and Elijah Wood were Brava and Studio 9. Sean Bean frequented Molly Malone's while Viggo Mortensen was content with steak and chips at the Green Parrot.

New Zealand fashion also played its part; Liv Tyler has been pictured in international fashion magazines wearing Zambesi, a leading New Zealand fashion label. She also shopped in the Wellington fashion design store Starfish.

The Hobbits found another means of relaxation at Lyall Bay, close to Wellington Airport, when first one and then another tried the art of surfing. Within hours all four could be seen riding the waves.

TOTALLY WELLINGTON

PIERRE VINET

Filmed at Fort Dorset in the suburb of Seatoun, this old army base is not accessible to the public. Nothing remains of the set but those wishing to obtain a view of the base can go to the end of Burnham Street and walk around the beach. This allows a good view without trespassing.

PIERRE VINET

The township of *Bree* was located near the intersection of the *East* and *North Roads* in central *Eriador*. A hamlet of both Hobbits and Men, the *Prancing Pony Inn* was the centre of community life for both the local populace and travellers who frequented the tavern each night to gossip and share stories. A two-day ride from *Hobbiton*, it became the overnight refuge for the four Hobbits as they fled their homeland.

It didn't feel like we were making a big film. It was all happening in Peter Jackson's back yard. His back yard, of course, being New Zealand, which has the most amazing landscapes and people necessary to bring it off.

Ian McKellen

IAN BRODIE

The set has been totally removed but for the curious, travel out on the Western Hutt Road to Haywards Hill Road. The quarry is at the bottom of this hill and is closed to the public.

PIERRE VINET

The fortress of *Helm's Deep* was located in the northern *White Mountains* at the head of the *Deeping Comb*. Although built by *Gondor* it was later occupied by the men of *Rohan* and became a refuge during times of war. *The Tower of the Hornburg*, *Helm's Gate*, the *Deeping Wall* and *Deeping Tower* were major fortifications guarding the *Aglarond*; a series of caverns reaching back into the hills. Also known as the *Glittering Caves*, these became a place of hiding during the *Battle of Helm's Deep*.

Ah, God bless Wellington! I love it so much.
I want to have a place there that I can go
and visit. It's wonderful. It's home.
I mean, I spent a year and a half
of my life there.

Elijah Wood

CENTRE STAGE

Above: The golden sands of Abel Tasman National Park.

Below: Taste Nelson wines and seafood at Mapua.

With a mild Mediterranean climate, Nelson is well known for its beautiful beaches and bush-clad mountains, and has become the centre for crafts, food and winemaking. Home to three national parks, people visit all year round to tramp, walk, sail and taste.

Nelson was first named Whakatu by Ra Kai Hau Tu, and in later years Pohea established the Matangi Awhio Pa on the edge of the harbour. In the nineteenth century, European settlers created their own piece of Victorian England, still evident today, with many fine old villas standing in streets named Hardy, Brönte, Haven and Wakefield.

The three national parks are easily accessible and offer diverse landscapes. Abel Tasman National Park is New Zealand's only coastal park. Beautiful golden sand beaches are a feature and there are opportunities to experience marine activities including sea kayaking, sailing, cruising and walking the popular Coast Track.

Nelson Lakes National Park is more mountainous and includes the northernmost peaks of the Southern Alps. The park features two gorgeous mountain lakes, with bush and alpine walks, horse treks and fishing trips. In winter visitors ski the Rainbow Valley, which also provides ski touring and alpine climbing.

The second largest national park in New Zealand, Kahurangi National Park, includes the largest remaining area of natural land in the northwestern South Island.

Filming was undertaken in three remote locations and some unique 'props' originated from local craftspeople.

The cast particularly enjoyed their time here, making the most of the idyllic beaches and calm seas.

CENTRE STAGE

INTERNET

www.NelsonNZ.com

With over 300 artisans in the region it was no wonder *The Lord of the Rings* prop department looked here for a number of props.

Situated in Richmond, Harrington Brewers were asked to brew a special beer for *Hobbiton* and the *Prancing Pony*. A number were tested before the crew settled on Harrington's Stout. This rich dark stout derives its character from a blend of toasted malts combined with a special strain of yeast. There was one other consideration — the brew had to have an alcohol content of no more than 1.1%. Due to the many takes required to perfect a shot, anything stronger could have had disastrous effects. The result was a good-looking and fine-tasting ale, and over 20,000 litres were provided. The brewery is open to the public and enthusiasts can purchase Harrington's Stout, with an added 5% alcohol by volume.

Above: Thorkild Hansen at work.

Below: The One Ring to rule them all.

Each year the Nelson World of Wearable Art Extravaganza showcases unique artworks all centred on one proviso — finished designs must be original, sometimes bizarre, certainly unique, and able to be worn. The World of Wearable Art and Collectable Cars, close to Nelson Airport, features a number of these innovative fashions, many designed by artists who worked on costumes for *The Lord of the Rings*.

Jens Hansen Gold and Silversmith is tucked away on Trafalgar Square in central Nelson. Amongst the jeweller's many designs one now eclipses all others. After submitting a design for the *One Ring* to the producers, Jens went on to make 40 rings, one almost 16 cm in diameter, with a similarly scaled gold chain. Sadly, Jens died in 1999 before he could see his masterpiece on screen but his son, Thorkild, continues the family tradition. One of the original rings is on display and Thorkild will craft copies of the *One Ring* in both 9 and 18 ct gold.

PIERRE VINET

INTERNET

www.worldofwearableart.co.nz

NEW LINE PRODUCTIONS

Fleeing from Bree and the horror of the Black Riders, the Hobbits are led by Aragorn into the Chetwood Forest, northeast of Bree.

Above: Frodo and Sam depart the Shire – little realising the adventures that would befall them.

Below: Forest and sinkholes – Takaka Hill.

Opposite: Rocky outcrops on Mt Olympus.

IAN BRODIE

The two-hour drive to this location is one of unspoilt beaches, striking mountain landscapes and dramatic holes in the earth. After passing through rich orchard areas a stop is recommended at Mapua to view the saltwater aquarium. The restaurant across the road serves great coffee and the freshest, tastiest smoked fish. With some fresh bread you now have a lunch to savour in the *Chetwood Forest*.

Pass through Motueka and pause at the golden sand beach of Kaiteriteri, where summer holiday-makers sunbathe and swim in the clear blue waters.

Climbing to the 972 m summit of the Takaka Hill, a number of rocky marble outcrops can be seen, the only place outside of Italy where such formations exist. Takaka marble can be seen in many public buildings (including Parliament House) throughout New Zealand.

Just past the signposted Ngarua Caves watch for the unpaved Canaan Road on your right, which will take you on an 11-km journey through ghostly trees amidst outcrops of weather-worn marble to the general location of filming. For the energetic, there is a two-hour return walk to Harward's Hole, a 176-m deep, 15-m wide tomo (sinkhole) in the limestone rock. The twelfth largest in the world and the largest in the southern hemisphere, it's very popular with potholers. *A note of warning*: keep to the marked paths in this area as a number of other unmarked sinkholes rival the best in *Moria*.

After returning to the main road continue to the summit of Takaka Hill for great views of Golden and Tasman Bays before winding downhill to Takaka, principal point of entry to Abel Tasman National Park. There are a number of scenic attractions in the area and you may wish to stay the night to fully appreciate them.

LOCATION
S40° 57.707—E172° 53.062

Two of the most spectacular landscapes in *The Fellowship of the Ring* are situated in Kahurangi National Park. The first, on the side of Mt Olympus, would not have appeared at all were it not for the local knowledge of Nelson Helicopters' pilot, Bill Reid. While filming was underway at Takaka, Bill described a place he thought would be ideal to show some of the rough country south of

IAN BRODIE

Rivendell. Several months later, when snow made filming at another location impossible, this became where the fellowship hide from Saruman's *crebain* (black crows from *Dunland*) who were searching for the Nine.

The location is remote and spectacular, and so isolated the only way for the average traveller to reach it is with the help of Nelson Helicopters. This company provided considerable logistical support to the crew while they filmed in the region and transported all the cast and crew from base camp to the cliff-top sites. Nelson Helicopters offer a number of scenic flights within the region and offer a special *Lord of the Rings* location tour that flies over the Chetwood Forest, Mt Olympus and Mt Owen — it is highly recommended.

Mt Olympus is appropriately named. The rocky outcrops sprout from the side of the mountain as if the gods themselves cast them there in some form of demented game. Over time, water has eroded away the softer rock to reveal a harder form, twisted and cracked into unbelievable columnar shapes. At times the valley below is covered in cloud and the stark pillars point to the sky in an accusing manner, adding to the mystical effect of this Olympian playground.

As members of the Fellowship cooked a meagre meal under the shelter of the rocks Merry and Pippin practised swordsmanship with Boromir. The keen eyes of Legolas spotted the approaching crebain and as the fire is hurriedly extinguished the Fellowship take cover to avoid detection.

IAN BRODIE

LOCATION	INTERNET
S40° 53.456—E172° 30.654	www.nelsonhelicopters.co.nz

Mt Olympus

south of Rivendell

New Line Productions

Ian Brodie

Ian Brodie

Ian Brodie

Dimrill Dale

The 1800 m peak of Mt Owen is situated near Murchison, at the southern end of Kahurangi National Park. This park contains some of the oldest rocks in New Zealand and many geological features found here link the area with the ancient continent of Gondwanaland.

IAN BRODIE

As the helicopter crosses the eastern slopes of Mt Owen, a bleached moonscape of glaciated marble karst is exposed and as you move closer the scale of the rocks is revealed. The seemingly flat features are split with crevasses and interspersed with deep sinkholes like the face of a wrinkled troll — an area that truly displays the awesome power of nature. As water has fallen on the soft limestone over millions of years, a vast underground drainage network has evolved, resulting in New Zealand's largest cave system.

When you see this location for yourself, you start to realise the immensity of the huge undertaking in filming *The Lord of the Rings*. Totally exposed to the elements, crew and actors were transported here by helicopter for ten days to complete filming, and the results are spectacular.

To portray the depleted Fellowship escaping from the horrors of *Moria*, wooden steps were built on the site and the eastern doors of *Moria* added digitally. It is a tribute to the location scouts that one of the most emotively charged scenes in *The Fellowship of The Ring* was geographically enhanced by the bleached moonscape of Mt Owen.

While it's possible to tramp to this site, it's not recommended for other than experienced mountaineers, so sit back, relax and enjoy a magic helicopter ride.

Opposite top: The keen eyes of the Sindarin elf Legolas spots the approaching Crebain.

Opposite middle left: The spot where the Fellowship hid from the crebain.

Opposite middle right: A Nelson Helicopters' Squirrel perches on the only flat ground.

Opposite bottom and this page: Surrealism in nature at Mt Olympus.

IAN BRODIE

LOCATION
S41° 33.493—E172° 32.401

Mt Owen
Dimrill Dale

Ian Brodie

New Line Production

Ian Brodie

Ian Brodie

'Never shall I forget the utter loneliness of the prospect — only the little far away homestead giving sign of human handiwork, the vastness of mountain and plain, of river and sky; the marvellous atmospheric affects — sometimes black mountains against a white sky, and then again, after cold weather, white mountains against a black sky.' Thus wrote Samuel Butler in

IAN BRODIE

his classic novel *Erewhon*, a fine description of a harsh landscape that for eleven months became *Edoras*, the capital city of *Rohan*. Situated in a large mountain valley, the treeless golden tussock land of Erewhon, with its shingle-sloped alpine peaks providing a jagged backdrop, is a lonely prospect.

The closest town is Methven, 85 km to the northeast on the edge of the Canterbury Plains. In summer the town basks in 30°C heat caused by the hot northwest wind, playground for Cantabrians who jet boat the nearby rivers, picnic in the shade and barbecue Canterbury lamb, of which they are justifiably proud. In winter skiers descend to occupy the many lodges, frequent the local bars and ski nearby Mt Hutt, one of the finest fields in New Zealand. The cast and crew occupied most of the accommodation here during filming and enjoyed the local hospitality.

Leaving Methven the road runs parallel to the Southern Alps across broad plains before reaching Mt Somers. Make a right turn here, and the unpaved road passes through the Ashburton Gorge and skirts the clear trout-stocked Lakes Camp and Clearwater, before climbing steadily to a view that takes your breath away as the broad valley of the Rangitata River and Erewhon is dramatically revealed.

Opposite top: A helicopter indicates the scale of the landscape.

Opposite middle left: Sam overcome with emotion at the loss of Gandalf in Moria.

Opposite middle right: Helicopter approach to Mt Owen.

Opposite bottom: Small crevasses reach deep into the mountain.

Above: Mt Sunday appears in the distant centre.

Below: The Riders of Rohan depart their capital, Edoras.

INTERNET

www.ChristchurchNZ.net

PIERRE VINET

PIERRE VINET

Above: The remaining members of the Fellowship arrive at Edoras.

Opposite: Meduseld had been standing for 450 years by the time of the War of the Ring.

Edoras (the Courts) was the capital of Rohan and comprised a number of dwellings encircling a central hill housing the King's hall, Meduseld. The roof and pillars of Meduseld were covered with pure gold, and it was also known as the Golden Hall of Edoras. Completed in 2569 (TA), it lay at the feet of the White Mountains near the River Snowbourn.

Born high up in the spectacular Southern Alps, the Rangitata River is created by snow-fed tributaries and forms an alluvial shingle fan, with an associated large valley, virtually surrounded by towering mountains. Within this basin the terminal moraine of ancient glaciers have created rocky outcrops that seem to sprout from the shingle. One of these, Mt Sunday, was used to create *Edoras* and *Meduseld, King Theoden's* hall, in Tolkien's realm of *Rohan*, the land of fabled horses and valiant warriors.

Descending into the Rangitata Valley Mt Sunday can be seen straight ahead, surrounded by brown tussock and tributaries of the braided river. There is no access to the mountain itself and the best views are obtained on the unpaved road as it passes the entrance to Mt Potts Station.

One of the more elaborate sets, *Edoras*, took eleven months to complete and created great interest with many Cantabrians who, armed with binoculars and cameras, travelled in over the weekends to catch a glimpse of the magnificent edifice. A cheeky newspaper journalist hired a light aircraft to fly over the area, obtaining a photographic scoop, with the images published worldwide.

Mt Potts is a high country station of 2700 ha and stretches from an altitude of 500 m to 2300 m. Approximately 70% is summer hill country and home to hardy New Zealand merino sheep. Accommodation in an alpine lodge or cottages on the station provides the perfect opportunity to experience life in the high country with a restaurant providing delicious home-cooked meals after a day of tramping, fishing or just quietly reading a book.

INTERNET:	VIEWPOINT OF *EDORAS:* S43° 34.852—E170° 58.212
www.mtpotts.co.nz	*EDORAS:* S43° 32.899—E170° 53.591

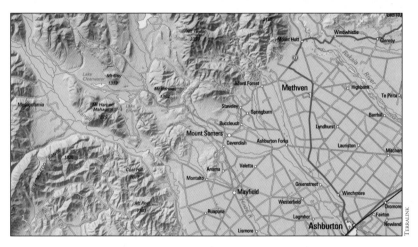

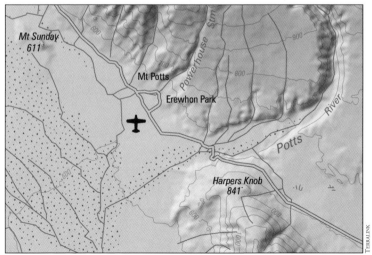

the flight to the ford

The Great East Road is a lonely road to travel. During the Third Age Dwarves mainly used it as they travelled from the Misty Mountains to their mines in the Blue Mountains. Stretching from Rivendell in the East to Lindon and the Grey Havens in the West, the road was the only course available to Arwen as she rushed Frodo towards the Ford of Bruinen and the relative safety of Rivendell.

Ian Brodie

Pierre Vinet

Tarras is a small farming village situated at the southern end of the Lindis Pass (970.4 m) linking the McKenzie Basin with Central Otago. The Lindis Pass follows a Maori trail used by the Ngai Tahu, who travelled from the Waitaki River Basin to Lakes Wanaka and Hawea for summer fishing. John Turnbull Thomson found the trail in 1857 and in 1871 the brown hills became home to the first red deer liberated in Otago. An area of stark beauty, it is particularly photogenic in the late evening, as the setting sun turns the hills into distinct shades of brown.

In Tarras you'll find a general store, petrol station, souvenir shop, bookshop and a coffee shop, which is a great place to stop for a while. The Tarras area also offers the opportunity to stay on a merino sheep farm, an interesting alternative to a hotel or motel.

The *Great East Road* is a ten-minute drive away. Although the scenes from *The Fellowship of the Ring* were filmed on private land, much can still be seen from the road. Travel south towards Cromwell for approximately 6 km then turn right onto the unsealed Maori Point Road. After travelling a further 2 km you'll be in the area used as the *Great East Road* and to portray the *Flight to the Ford,* with filming carried out through the pine forests.

Continuing along Maori Point Road it's possible to take some excellent shots of the Southern Alps, used as the *Misty Mountains* surrounding *Rivendell.* The Clutha River can also be glimpsed to the left of the road. The largest river in New Zealand, it's slightly shorter than the Waikato River in the North Island but discharges almost twice the volume of water. The Maori name for the Clutha is Mata-au, which means surface current. The river was named by Scottish settlers after the Clyde River in Scotland (Clutha being Gaelic for Clyde) and proved to be a rich source of gold. At the beginning of the twentieth century over 150 dredges worked the river.

Now one of the fastest growing areas in New Zealand, Lake Wanaka makes for a pleasant stopover. Of note are two unique attractions — the eccentric Stuart Landsborough's Puzzling World & Great Maze and the World War II fighter aircraft at the NZ Fighter Pilots' Museum. Nearby, Hawea Flat is home to the Flying Trestles, caterers to Mr Jackson, the crew and stars.

PIERRE VINET

Looking towards the Alps from the Wanaka waterfront, at the end of the lake you can see the backdrop used when *Gandalf* flew to *Rohan* with *Gwaihir,* after his rescue from *Orthanc.*

Another location is on the road marked Glendhu Bay and Treble Cone Ski Field. After approximately 15 km you pass Glendhu Bay on your right. Continue towards Treble Cone and just before the ski field turn-off you'll reach a view of the location. On the large brown hill on your right a ruined structure was digitally imposed and used in an aerial sequence, as the *Fellowship* headed south.

Returning to Wanaka, take State Highway 89 to Queenstown. The road soon starts to climb through the Cardrona Valley. Near the entrance to the Cardrona Ski Field and Waiorau Snow Farm stands the Cardrona Hotel, one of New Zealand's oldest. When you enter the bar, the *Prancing Pony* at *Bree* immediately comes to mind; looking into the corners you might expect to see a solitary *Ranger* puffing silently on a pipe, or a swarthy Easterner about to ask if your surname is *Baggins.* Accommodation and meals are available at the hotel.

Following the Cardrona River, the road climbs steadily towards the 1119.7 m summit where you can park your car and explore.

NEW LINE PRODUCTIONS

Opposite top: The Great East Road stretching through the pines.

Opposite bottom: Arwen and Frodo flee the Nazgûl.

Above top: A good mug of beer and food satisfy the Hobbits' appetite at The Prancing Pony, Bree.

Above: Ancient ruins in the rough country south of Rivendell.

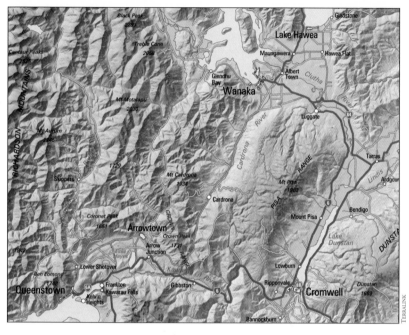

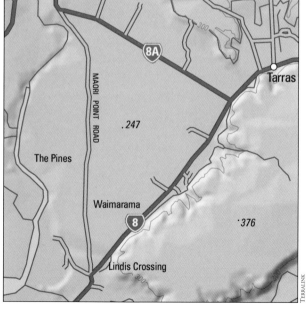

Top: The Crown Range route.

Left: Tarras and the Great East Road region.

Opposite: Glendhu Bay.

IAN BRODIE

The view is expansive; to the left are the *River Anduin* and the *Pillars of the Argonath,* and high in the hills (straight ahead) is the *Dimrill Dale.* Now travel downhill another kilometre and make another stop. To the right is the *Ford of Bruinen* and in the far distance *Amon Hen* can be seen, nestled on the shore of *Nen Hithoel.* This area was also used for publicity stills of the Fellowship as they headed south in the rough country of *Eregion.*

'The road goes ever on' in a series of tight curves,

PIERRE VINET

Above top: A welcome stop at Glendhu Bay.

Above: The Fellowship in Eregion.

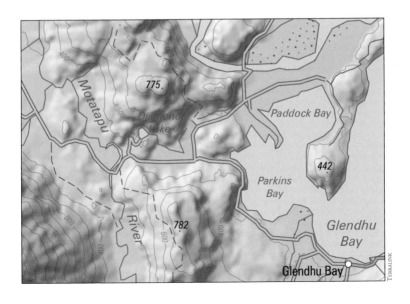

TERRALINK

59

IAN BRODIE

Above: Near Treble Cone.

Below: The expansive view from the top of the Crown Range, looking towards Queenstown.

Below bottom: The rough country south of Rivendell.

IAN BRODIE

IAN BRODIE

before reaching a shelf of rich farmland with brown hills frowning on the right. There is another steep, downward spiral and six hairpin turns to negotiate to reach the valley floor. Turn left for a short drive to the *Pillars of the Kings*, a glass of fine Central Otago wine and the opportunity to throw oneself off a bridge into the *River Anduin* — attached to a bungy, of course!

After 5 km the Kawarau River is crossed, and immediately on your left is the headquarters of A.J. Hackett Bungy. An adventure born in Vanuatu and developed in New Zealand, bungy jumping has spread to all corners of the world. A.J. Hackett and speed skier, Henry Van Asch, developed the idea of jumping from a great height with an elastic bungy cord attached to their legs after watching videos of experiments by the Oxford University Dangerous Sports Club. In 1987 Hackett's jump from the Eiffel Tower created tremendous interest (and notoriety) for the new sport. In November 1988, the historic Kawarau Suspension Bridge became the world's first 'bungy bridge'. There are now six different bungy sites to jump from in the Queenstown area, including the 134-m high Nevis Highwire, which Orlando Bloom and crew tried out when they worked in the region.

Pillars of the Kings

Immediately opposite A.J. Hackett's bungy jump is the entrance road to Chard Farm Vineyard and a spectacular view of the *Anduin* and *Argonath* (*Sindarin 'Pillars of the Kings'*).

Although the Pillars were computer-generated into each side of the river, the area is instantly recognisable.

Continuing along this short road you come to one of the founding vineyards in Central Otago. At latitude 45° South, Central Otago is perched on the southern edge of the grape-growing world. The northern hemisphere equivalent would run from Bordeaux to Southern Spain.

Chard Farm was established in 1987 and was one of the first commercial vineyards in the Southern Lakes District. Since then the area has become one of the biggest wine producers in New Zealand, with four sub-regions. The altitude and climate have distinct characteristics —you'll find New Zealand's highest vineyard above sea-level and the furthest vineyard from the sea. The continental climate gives warm, dry summers, cool autumns and cold winters, with relatively low humidity. The large diurnal temperature range helps seal in flavours and acids in white wines and encourages colour development in Pinot Noir. Cellar door sales at Chard Farm are available seven days from 10 a.m. to 5 p.m. Winery tours are by appointment only.

A further 2 km towards Cromwell you'll find Gibbston Valley Wines, boasting a popular restaurant, an adjacent cheese factory, and a unique and innovative wine cave. Dug 76 m into the Central Otago schist, tours are available daily between 10 a.m. and 4 p.m. Each tour culminates in the cave, where both Gibbston Valley Chardonnay and Pinot Noir can be tasted and enjoyed in unique surroundings.

The two huge carved likenesses of Isildur and Anárion in the chasm of the Anduin were built during the Third Age by Rómendacil of Gondor to mark the northern entrance to that realm.

Below: Kawarau River with Chard Farm in the distance.

Below bottom: The Fellowship rafted from the bungy bridge.

IAN BRODIE

IAN BRODIE

PILLARS OF THE KINGS

S 45° 00.711'—E 168° 53.567'

The Kawarau River
rafting the Anduin

PIERRE VINET

With a length of over 1300 miles, the River Anduin is the longest in Middle-earth. From Mirkwood in the north to Gondor in the south, it flowed past many regions before finally spreading out into a broad delta and entering the sea through the Ethir Anduin, south of Dol Amroth. The Fellowship spent eleven days paddling downstream from Lothlórien, covering a distance of almost 300 miles to the breaking of the Fellowship at Amon Hen.

The chance to raft down the *Anduin* is certainly an opportunity not to be missed and comes highly recommended. Local company Extreme Green Rafting worked with Peter Jackson for two years, providing all the rafting equipment and expertise for the river sequences. They now offer two trips down the *Anduin*: one includes some action-packed rafting, the other is a 'softer' option, which doesn't require wetsuits, for the less adventurous. Both trips float you past the location of the *Argonath*. Reservations can be made by calling their office in nearby Queenstown and transfers are provided from the town centre.

The Kawarau River flows from its source at Lake Wakatipu to Cromwell, where it joins the Clutha River at Lake Dunstan. The Kawarau Gorge was once a rich source of gold and you can see and experience how the miners of olden days lived at the Goldfields Mining Centre, a further 15 km towards Cromwell. Here you can take a guided tour of the diggings and an exhilarating jet-boat ride down the river.

Back on the road towards Queenstown and approximately 1 km past the Crown Range exit, turn right towards Arrowtown and the *Ford of Bruinen*.

PIERRE VINET

INTERNET
www.extremegreenrafting.com

the Ford of Bruinen

Located a scenic twenty-minute drive from Queenstown, Arrowtown promotes itself as 'Born of Gold'. In 1862 William Fox discovered one of the world's richest gold-bearing areas here, and in the ensuing gold rush over 7000 Europeans and Chinese came seeking alluvial gold in the nearby Arrow and Shotover Rivers. The bustling community had its share of lawlessness and notorious gangsters and thugs descended on the gold fields to make a living by various nefarious means. The excellent Lakes District Centennial Museum situated on the narrow one-way main street provides a wealth of information about the area, including the many characters who worked the gold fields.

DESTINATION QUEENSTOWN

Opposite top and bottom: The small Elven boats approach the Argonath on the River Anduin.

Above: Lake Hayes, near Queenstown.

Below: Miners' cottage near Arrowtown.

Here autumn is especially wonderful; the tree-lined main street becomes a leafy carpet of red and gold as smoke from the chimneys of the original miners' cottages creates a hazy atmosphere in shafts of sunlight. Larches interspersed with pines on the nearby hills create golden pools of colour and the air is clear and crisp with the crackle of frost in the morning confirming another breathtaking day. Many of Arrowtown's shops and galleries feature the work of local artists, so take your time to browse and don't forget your camera.

Restored Chinese miners' cottages can be viewed via a short walk from the main street, an interesting reminder of Arrowtown's past.

Nearby the world-famous Millbrook Resort features luxurious accommodation and restaurants surrounded by a par-72 world championship golf course, designed by Sir Bob Charles, New Zealand's renowned master golfer.

DESTINATION QUEENSTOWN

INTERNET

www.queenstownnz.co.nz

Arrowtown
the Ford of Bruinen

PIERRE VINET

The Ford of Rivendell was located where the Great East Road crossed the River Bruinen (Sindarin 'Loudwater'). Under the power of Elrond it could be raised at will to stop any unwanted visitors and provided the last bastion of defence into the Hidden Valley.

The *Ford* is only minutes from the centre of the village on the Arrow River. Park in the area behind the main street and walk down to the adjacent riverbank.

To reach the exact spot walk upstream for some 200 m, which can involve wading the river (normally only ankle deep). This will place you in the direction the *Nazgûl* charged as *Arwen* ferried *Frodo* across the river on *Asfaloth,* her Elven steed. The path the *Nazgûl* took down to the river is clearly visible on your left.

The scene showing the flooding of the river was filmed in the Shotover River at Skippers Canyon (see next page). One of the more 'public' locations, during the three days spent filming here many locals lined the riverbank to watch. The local Saffron Restaurant became one of the cast's favourite dinner locations.

You can still fossick for gold here and stores on the main street hire pans to enable a search for gold and a means of recovering your holiday costs.

The magical flood *Arwen* invoked to dispel the *Nazgûl* had an eerie echo in reality, with a genuine flash flood washing away part of the set during filming of *The Fellowship of the Ring.*

FORD OF BRUINEN
S 44° 56.147'—E 168° 49.863'

IAN BRODIE

Turning now to Queenstown, you'll soon see the Coronet Peak ski area on your right. There is an access road closer to Queenstown. The sealed road is designed to transport skiers in the winter months but is open all year round and a most imposing view of the Wakatipu Basin can be obtained from the car park, 1188 m above sea level.

NEW LINE PRODUCTIONS

Skiing and snowboarding are popular during winter months and every year increasing numbers of visitors from around the world descend on the Southern Lakes Region to enjoy the spectacular conditions. There are five ski fields within 90 minutes' drive of Queenstown, catering for all levels of ability.

The Coronet Peak road also provides access to Skippers Canyon, where you can stop and admire the view at the turn-off. However, for many visitors the preferred choice is to travel into the Canyon with one of the local 4WD operators. The road is closed to rental cars and can be quite tortuous in places, especially for drivers not familiar with these sorts of roads.

In its heyday, Skippers was the most prolific of the local gold fields, with each square foot of its bed said to hold an ounce of gold. It is well worth a guided tour into the canyon and down to the river itself. The steep valley walls, winding road, stark brown hills and contrasting snow-covered peaks alone are worth the visit, but of equal interest is the river itself. The part of the river close to the original bridge (approximately 12 km into the gorge) was used to portray the *Ford of Bruinen* in flood, one of the most dramatic and memorable scenes from *The Fellowship of the Ring*.

Opposite top: The sight of the nine Nazgûl together would terrify the most stouthearted.

Opposite bottom: Paddle through the Arrow River to the Ford of Bruinen.

Above: Arwen turns to face the Nazgûl at the Ford of Bruinen.

Below: Helicopter view of the ford in Skippers Canyon.

IAN BRODIE

FORD OF BRUINEN (SKIPPERS)
S44° 50' 808—E168° 40' 936

DESTINATION QUEENSTOWN

Above: Queenstown with the Remarkables on the right.

Opposite top: The remote and lonely country encountered by the Fellowship.

Opposite bottom: The icy waters of Lake Alta.

> *I recalled sitting in Queenstown against the mountain range aptly titled the Remarkables and feeling I was actually living the books. It was like Tolkien had walked across New Zealand.*
>
> Sean Astin

Queenstown is one of New Zealand's most well-known and popular tourist destinations. Nestled in an alpine valley alongside Lake Wakatipu, it's good enough for all the tourist clichés to ring true.

Maori legend tells of a tipua (demon) who seized a beautiful girl. Rescued by her lover while the demon slept, the hero set fire to the area and as the flames licked the demon's body he drew his knees upwards in pain. The enormous amount of fat in his body fanned the fire and a large chasm was dug as he writhed. Rain and snow extinguished the fire, but the demon was destroyed — all except for his heart. Today, the shape of the lake reveals his outline, while his beating heart causes the lake to rise and fall.

The first Europeans to settle in the area were William Gilbert Rees and Paul von Tunzelmann. Cutting their way through the thorny undergrowth for weeks on end they arrived at Lake Wakatipu and decided to go no further. They settled their sheep in the remoteness, not realising their peaceful existence was about to change with William Fox's discovery of gold in the Arrow River. The population exploded and Queenstown became the major service centre supplying the miners.

Tourism is now the 'goldmine' and visitors from around the world descend on Queenstown, also known as The Adventure Capital of New Zealand.

The cast and crew fell in love with the area, with the *Hobbits* also finding plenty of time to explore the nightclubs and hotels. With the local High School doubling as audition headquarters, schoolteachers became *Orcs* and taxi drivers were transformed into the people of *Rohan*. At the height of casting over 500 people a day queued for their opportunity to enter Middle-earth.

PIERRE VINET

With a permanent population of just 11,000, Queenstown now hosts over 1 million visitors a year. The main street, closed to traffic, is a mecca for those who like to sit in the sun and 'do coffee' with the imposing lake and mountain view offering a perfect backdrop. The sheer breadth of tourist activities is impossible to list but there is something for every taste and age, with a number of reservation offices offering excellent advice.

A trip on the grand old lady of the lake is a highlight. The steamer *Earnslaw* recently celebrated her ninetieth anniversary, having been assembled in 1912 to provide transportation from the railhead at Kingston. Just over 50 m in length and with a beam of 7.3 m, the stately steamer now operates a number of tourist excursions on Lake Wakatipu. The cruise to Walter Peak offers distant views of *Amon Hen* (Closeburn).

PIERRE VINET

Even though we are right down here at the bottom of the world we have mountains, forests and fields, rivers, lakes and waterfalls that have a familiar yet slightly fantastical appearance.

Peter Jackson

The ascent of Bob's Peak by gondola provides a breathtaking view. One of the steepest cableways in the world, it rises some 446 m over a distance of 731 m. There is a fully licensed restaurant at the top providing one of the most romantic viewpoints for dinner in the world.

Queenstown can be visited and enjoyed all year round, snow falling in the town in winter provides a white blanket to excite skiers, while summer temperatures reach over 30° Celsius.

Allocate at least three days here to fully appreciate the film locations. Also, take some time to visit the Rattlesnake Bar and Rydges Hotel, both used by the cast as watering holes.

DESTINATION QUEENSTOWN

Ian Brodie

Chris Coad

Deer Park Heights is located at Kelvin Heights, off the main road to Te Anau and less than twenty minutes' drive from Queenstown. After passing the airport entrance and crossing the Kawarau River, take the road on the right marked Kelvin Heights. The entrance is a further 5 km on your left.

Deer Park Heights is an 800-m conical hill and its top is one giant movie set with a number of walks revealing many other locations, all with panoramic views. Looking north over the airport the *River Anduin* can be seen flowing towards the *Pillars of the Kings*. Its inhabitants also allow visitors a close encounter with tame llamas, deer, goats and bison.

The hillside was used for locations in all three films and because of its proximity to Queenstown, it was utilised for many 'pick-up' shots.

Take the unpaved road to the top of the hill and you'll be confronted by a Korean prison used as a set in the 1986 film *The Rescue*. From here a number of locations are easily accessible. The first is a track running a few metres to the left of the road by the prison, heading south, where *Gandalf* was photographed for publicity shots.

The second is a small mountain tarn 500 m south of the car park. Here a short sequence was filmed depicting *Gandalf* riding to *Minas Tirith* on the *West Road* to *Gondor*. The distant mountains were digitally enhanced. Walking to the other side of the tarn reveals another scene — the refugees from *Rohan* escaping with the Remarkables as a backdrop.

Return to the car park, walk around the other side of the prison and you'll find where *Éowyn* provided *Aragorn* with his 'tasty' stew.

MOUNTAIN TARN
S 45° 02.456'—E 168° 43.700'

Ian Brodie

The movie sequence showing a depleted and demoralised Fellowship fleeing from their ordeal in the terrifying *Mines of Moria* without *Gandalf* was filmed in two locations at opposite ends of the South Island. After the Fellowship gathers their composure, *Aragorn* leads them down the steep slopes of the *Dimrill Dale* towards *Lothlórien*. This location is situated high in the Remarkables Ranges and can be reached by one of two different routes.

PIERRE VINET

The energetic can drive to the top of the Remarkables Ski Field, which is situated 20 km from Queenstown. Upon reaching the car park the alpine tarn of Lake Alta is a further 20-minute hike up the hill. A reasonable level of fitness is required.

By far the easier option (and easily the more exciting) is to take a helicopter flight with local company Heliworks, who were responsible for providing helicopters and pilots for most of the aerial filming and transportation for the entire trilogy. Experts in their field, they now know this part of Middle-earth intimately, and their experienced pilots Alfie Speight and Dennis Egerton can transport you directly to the many locations centered around Queenstown.

PIERRE VINET

The company offers three *Lord of the Rings* flights ranging from a 15-minute excursion to Lake Alta, *Amon Hen* and the *Ford of Bruinen* through to a 90-minute aerial extravaganza covering all the local locations. Flying like *Gwaihir* around the Southern Alps on your own Middle-earth adventure is a very special experience, and one that comes highly recommended as a climax to any tour of Middle-earth New Zealand.

Above top: The depleted Fellowship hurry down the Dimrill Dale to the safety of Lothlórien.

Opposite top: A small tarn at Deer Park Heights.

Opposite bottom: This tarn provided a number of locations.

INTERNET	DIMRILL DALE
www.heliworks.co.nz	S45° 3' 706—E168° 48' 868

Pierre Vinet

Heliworks will fly you directly to a landing point high above this point and from here wonderful photographs can be obtained of the *Dimrill Dale* and *Celebrant*.

Lake Alta is a typical alpine tarn. In winter it's frozen and covered with snow while in summer hardy sun-baked alpine plants eke out a living from the sparse soil under the schist rock. Schist is a metamorphic rock common to the mountains of the South Island, and formed when rocks deep within the earth are affected by heat or great pressure. Akin to slate, it's crumbly by nature and can be easily split along its many bands. A popular building material, it clads many fine homes in the Southern Lakes region.

A deep valley extending from the western doorway of the Mines of Moria, the Dimrill Dale was known by the Dwarves as Azanulbizar and as Nanduhirion by the Elves. The door itself was more correctly called the Dimrill Gate. Descending steeply the path skirted the Mirrormere (Dwarvish 'Kheled-zâram'), one of the Dwarves' most sacred places. Legend told of Durin the Deathless looking into the still deep waters to see his head crowned by seven stars — thus confirming his royalty. From its source in the Dimrill Dale, the Celebrant (Sindarin 'Silver-course' and also known as the Silverlode River) followed the valley and thence through Lothlórien .

Ian Brodie

Opposite top: Aragorn crosses
the River Silverlode.

Opposite bottom: Lake Alta
after an early autumn
snowfall.

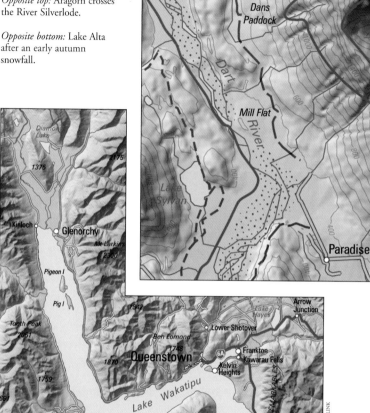

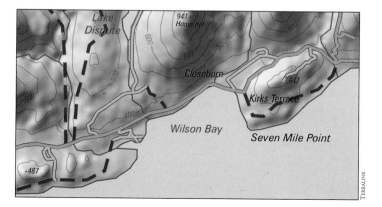

PIERRE VINET

Amon Hen (Sindarin 'The Hill of the Eye') was built by the men of Númenor as a watch-house to mark the northern border of Gondor. One of three tall hills on both sides of the Anduin and the Falls of Rauros, its companions were Amon Lhâw (Sindarin 'The Hill of the Ear') on the eastern bank and Tol Brandir (the Tindrock) in the middle of the river.

Above: Orcs approach Amon Hen.

Below: An aerial view of the Closeburn Peninsula.

IAN BRODIE

The scenic drive to Glenorchy follows the shores of Lake Wakatipu for 45 km. At times the road climbs around high bluffs with extended views of the lake and mountains, at others it passes secluded bays at lake-level. Pine trees cover the lower mountains in places and there are some lovely DOC-maintained walkways. Have your fishing rod handy, brown and rainbow trout cruise close to the shore in search of food — Viggo Mortensen was spotted many times fly-fishing in this area, although remember to organise a fishing licence first.

Closeburn is situated 8 km from Queenstown. While the actual location of *Amon Hen* is not accessible, a stop on the lakeshore is suggested, after descending the hill to Closeburn Bay. The area used for filming was set amongst the pine trees on the peninsula on your left, and the use of multiple sites to portray one scene is very apparent here. Filming for the climatic finale of *The Fellowship of the Ring* was undertaken at Closeburn, Paradise and Mavora Lakes, with the skill of the filmmakers weaving these three places together seamlessly.

In summer, Closeburn is an ideal barbecue area, very reminiscent of the scented forests of *Ithilien*. St John's wort and sweet briar roses send out their distinctive perfumes and provide a riot of colour that contrasts superbly with the abundant cream and white foxgloves.

The scent of pine trees and dramatic views of lake and mountains combine to truly bring *Ithilien* and Middle-earth into reality, so it's little wonder that nearby Twelve Mile Delta (see next page) was used to portray the *Ithilien Camp*.

AMON HEN
S45° 03' 562—E168° 33' 804

Ithilien Camp

PIERRE VINET

Situated 4 km past Closeburn is Twelve Mile Delta, an area of regenerating native bush complete with a mountain stream hurrying on its way to Lake Wakatipu. Managed by DOC, there is a large camping area available and a number of walks and mountain bike tracks will take you into *Ithilien Camp*. It makes an ideal camping or picnic spot with wonderful views of the surrounding mountains and bush. There are additional tracks a little further along the main road on the right.

Two areas were used here to portray the camp, one on the lower bank and the other on the higher plateau.

Above: Deep in thought, Faramir surveys Ithilien.

Below: Mountain stream of Twelve Mile Delta.

Here Frodo and Sam rested after the horror of the Black Gate, and witnessed a fierce battle on the upper ridge and saw the legendary mûmak.

The people of Harad waged war against Gondor almost continuously during the Third Age. Their land lay to the south and was divided into a number of small fiefdoms, all eager to lay claim to Gondor. The dark-skinned men of Harad were adept warriors and used a number of techniques to attack, including mûmakil, pachyderms of immense size complete with war-towers on their backs.

IAN BRODIE

IAN BRODIE

Above: The Wizard's Vale – Glenorchy and the Dart River.

Below: The Arcadia Guesthouse.

Opposite: The Tower of Orthanc nestled in Nan Curunír.

The little village of Glenorchy nestles at the northern end of Lake Wakatipu with the jagged peaks of the snow-capped *Misty Mountains* acting as a spectacular backdrop.

Maori passed through this area in their search for pounamu (jade or greenstone as it is known locally) but it wasn't until 1862 that settlers arrived, using the broad river flats for grazing. Some 3000 gold miners soon followed but yields proved less spectacular than in other regions, and they soon left. Tourism evolved in the 1890s and a number of guesthouses were built for adventurous European visitors travelling up the lake from Queenstown. The discovery of scheelite (used to make weapons grade tungsten) in 1905 saw over 50 workers extracting the ore until the 1980s. Today, Glenorchy has a population of just over 200 and has evolved into a centre for eco-tourism.

Glenorchy is also a gateway to Mt Aspiring National Park, covering 355,543 hectares and part of Te Wahipounamu (Southwest New Zealand World Heritage Area). A DOC information centre in the village provides information on the many outstanding walks, including the Routeburn Track, the Dart/ Rees and Greenstone/ Caples Valley tracks.

Accommodation ranges from backpacker to luxury and the Glen Roydon Lodge provides good food and excellent accommodation at reasonable prices. It became the local hangout for the crew and the proprietor, Eileen Todd, speaks proudly of her morning coffee with Peter Jackson and her time on the set of *Amon Hen*.

A couple of days can easily be spent in the area, walking, jet boating and horse trekking to *Isengard*, *Amon Hen* and *Lothlórien*.

DART RIVER JETBOAT SAFARIS

Isengard

NEW LINE PRODUCTIONS

Take the road marked Paradise. After some 15 km the magnificent Arcadia guesthouse appears on your left. Continuing on the open river flats give way to patches of beech forest. The native beech contains a number of different sub-species so while red beech flourishes in frost-free areas, silver beech happily grows in areas covered by winter snow. Although one might easily consider Paradise aptly named for its tranquillity, it is, in fact, named for the Paradise ducks in the area. Nearby Diamond Lake is well stocked with rainbow and brown trout.

After a further 5 km a large green field (Dan's Paddock) appears on the right, where Weta Studios added *Isengard*. Standing by the paddock one can easily imagine *Isengard* nestled into *Nan Curunír (the Wizard's Vale)* with the mighty peak of *Methedras* (Mt Earnslaw) towering over the valley.

The area where the paddock and the forest meet was used to show the Fellowship entering *Lothlórien*. Past this point the terrain becomes rough and small streams must be forded. The preferred option is one of the excursions operated by Dart River Safaris and Dart Stables. The guides themselves are another special part of the journey — many worked on the film and have interesting experiences to relate.

A fortress built by the Dúnedain of Gondor at the height of their power, the Ring of Isengard contained the Tower of Orthanc (Sindarin 'Forked Height'), built of an unbreakable black rock and rising 500 feet above the plain. Deserted during the Third Age by the men of Gondor, it was reoccupied by Saruman the White, who destroyed the lush gardens and had it fortified. Underneath the ring he built many armouries and pits to house his countless armies of Orcs. The Ents destroyed Isengard during the War of the Ring but the tower survived because of its impregnable rock, and was retaken by Gondor in the Fourth Age.

TOWER OF ORTHANC
S44° 40' 220—E168° 20' 276

DART RIVER JETBOAT SAFARIS

Above: A Dart River Safaris' jet boat thunders down the Dart.

Below: The golden eaves of Lothlórien.

Opposite top: The proud Boromir, son of Denethor II meets his doom at Amon Hen.

Opposite bottom: Paradise on earth — on a Dart Stables' overnight horse trek.

Glenorchy-based Dart River Safaris operate both half and full day tours into the Dart River Valley by jet boat and funyak canoe, providing an ideal opportunity to explore *Isengard, Lothlórien* and *Amon Hen.* They also provide transfers from Queenstown.

The adventure starts with a 45-minute back road journey into the depths of the mountains. Passing *Isengard,* several stops are made before a 20-minute bush walk to the jet boat. This area has a magical quality — reminiscent of the *Old Forest* or *Mirkwood the Great,* the trees appear to have a permanence of thousands of years. To complete the scene small rivulets of water trickle through the mossy walls with the only other sound that of the Dart River rushing over sandy gravel.

All this is merely an entrée for the exciting 90-minute jet-boat ride. Heading further up river initially, the surrounding mountains envelop you as you skim over the narrow shallows. Frequent stops are made and your driver will demonstrate the jet boat's capability, including the famous 'Hamilton Turn'. Returning to Glenorchy, the river broadens into many braids and a stop is made close to the area of bush portrayed as *Amon Hen* where Merry and Pippin were captured by Orcs.

PIERRE VINET

INTERNET

www.dartriverjet.co.nz

PIERRE VINET

One of the most magical adventures in the area is a horse trek with Dart Stables. From Glenorchy there are options to suit both novice and experienced riders, including the highly recommended two-day trek, which passes by two film locations, taking you close to *Lothlórien* and the hillside of *Amon Hen*.

Trotting along beside the river, the path takes you closer to the mountains before entering the primeval beech forest. The destination for the night is a well-maintained hut in a clearing surrounded by a verdant patch of native bush, shown in the movie as the site where the Fellowship are met by *Haldir* and taken to *Galadriel*.

This area is one of the most exquisite locations in New Zealand. Dappled sunlight filters through the trees illuminating the luxuriant moss underfoot and dry leaves gather in drifts in every undulation. It is the perfect vision of *Lothlórien*.

After dinner by candlelight there is time to relax and experience an invigorating splash in the waterfall plunge pool. Sitting under the stars beside the roaring open fire the transportation to Middle-earth is complete and it would come as no surprise if *Gildor Inglorion* and his Elven kindred quietly joined you for food and drink.

Here at the edge of Lothlórien, relieved at their escape from Moria but filled with sorrow at the death of Gandalf, the Fellowship are met and taken to Galadriel. A short walk through the bush nearby is Amon Hen where Boromir finally succumbed to Lurtz, before the huge Orc met his own end at the hand of Aragorn.

IAN BRODIE

INTERNET

www.glenorchy.co.nz

PIERRE VINET

Above: Elven princesses in the ethereal light of Lothlórien.

Opposite top: Gandalf the White with Shawdowfax at the edge of Fangorn Forest.

Opposite bottom: Aragorn, Legolas and Gimli sift through the Orc ashes.

PIERRE VINET

It was an ideal, magical environment for the story, so it was that much easier to get lost in the illusion. I loved being there and I look forward to going back. It's a wonderful place.

Viggo Mortensen

Leaving Queenstown take the main route to Arrowtown passing Arthur's Point and one of the oldest hotels in New Zealand. The road then crosses the Edith Cavel Bridge, where below on the left is the departure point for the Shotover Jet. Operating high-powered jet boats down the river, they offer a spectacular ride.

In Arrowtown take the road down to the Arrow River to view the *Ford of Bruinen*. The village makes a welcome coffee stop before taking the Cromwell road. At the main State Highway turn left and drive for 5 km before crossing the Kawarau River Bridge, where the entrance road to Chard Farm is on your right. A short distance up this road the *River Anduin* and location of the *Pillars of the Kings* can be seen below. A recommended lunch stop is Gibbston Valley Wines, just a little further down the main road on your right.

Return to Queenstown via Lake Hayes to Deer Park Heights. Climbing the hill, you can obtain a magnificent view and visit a number of locations.

Now travel back to Queenstown Airport for your 45-minute Middle-earth Helicopter Explorer Tour with Heliworks. Leaving the airport, you'll climb the steep slopes of the *Misty Mountains* to the *Dimrill Dale* and the *Gates of Khazad-dûm*. The source of the *River Silverlode* lies below and after a pause for photographs you cross towards *Amon Hen*. There are more opportunities for photographs before continuing westward to *Fangorn Forest* and a landing on top of *Dol Baran*, where the vista of *Nan Curunír* (Isengard and the *Tower of Orthanc*) unfolds. The great forests beckon and as you fly over the outskirts of *Lothlórien* and *Fangorn* the massive peaks of the *Misty Mountains* tower overhead. *Amon Hen* lies below, where *Lurtz* fought his final battle against *Aragorn, Boromir, Legolas* and *Gimli*. The return towards Queenstown is via the *Great River*.

PIERRE VINET

A visit to the Mavora Lakes is your passport to a special forested area containing two serene lakes. Their remoteness ensures you are guaranteed solitude with an opportunity to relax and recharge your holiday batteries.

The lakes are situated off the main Five Rivers — Te Anau highway, watch for the signposted road past Mossburn (there is also an access road closer to Te Anau).

From here it is a scenic 39-km, 45-minute drive on an unpaved road to *Fangorn Forest* and *Nen Hithoel*. After travelling 35 km and just prior to the turn off to Mavora Lakes, you'll see a gateway on your right and a repaired fence on your left. On your left is the edge of *Fangorn Forest* so step quietly and you may catch a glimpse of an *Ent* standing like a sentinel in the trees. It's hard to imagine that during filming over 160 people worked from the paddock on your right.

Climb the fence on your left and walk 250 m in a northwesterly direction. Here *Éomer* and the *Riders of Rohan* burnt the remains of the dead *Orcs* after their epic battle. The locality is just as you would imagine — a brown hillock with the edge of the deep forest just metres away.

Fangorn Forest was one of the oldest in Middle-earth. A remnant of the Great Forests that covered most of Eriador, it was home to one of the oldest species in Middle-earth – the Ent.

Grown from saplings in the First Age, over the countless years the trees grew to great height and maturity. Some areas of the forest contained deep dells that remained dark and ominous.

ORC MOUND
S45° 19' 968—E168° 10' 404

PIERRE VINET

Ian Brodie

A long oval lake, Nen Hithoel calmed the waters of the Anduin after their rush through the Argonath in preparation for their drop over the Falls of Rauros. After mooring their Elven boats on the western shore they lit a small fire and rested, not realising this day would mark the breaking of the Fellowship.

Accommodation here is limited to a DOC campsite at the south end of the North Mavora, and provides an ideal chance to experience the great New Zealand outdoors. Toilets, barbecues, picnic tables and rubbish collection are provided and water is obtained from the lake. Roads provide easy access to the lake, and New Zealand's benign flora and fauna make for safe camping. Food can be as simple as casting a rod into the lake (the fishing season is 1 October to 30 April) with fat brown trout cruising the food-rich shoreline. A fishing licence is required. For those with plenty of space in the car or campervan don't forget to pack the kayak and mountain bike.

North Mavora became the *Nen Hithoel (Sindarin 'Lake of Many Mists')* foreshore which marked the end of the Fellowship's journey down the *River Anduin*.

As the road passes the south end of North Mavora look for a park bench and a lone toilet. Park here and walk up the slope 150 m into the forest, looking for a large tree stump at the top of the ridge. Here *Merry* and *Pippin* hid from the *Orcs*, and the large tree shielded *Frodo* from the *Uruk-hai*. The slopes here were also used to portray *Lurtz* and his band running through the forest to *Nen Hithoel*.

Go back down to the lakeshore and walk 200 m north, to where the campfire was lit prior to the breaking of the Fellowship. It also marks the spot where *Frodo* and *Sam* were filmed crossing to the eastern shore for their journey to *Mordor*.

Put your hand into the lake and spare a thought for Sean Astin. After each take he changed into dry clothes, warmed himself by a large 'blower' heater and then did it all again.

TREE STUMP: S45° 16' 024—E168° 10' 500	
LAKESIDE CAMPFIRE: S45° 15' 993—E168° 10' 410	

Pierre Vinet

Silverlode River

IAN BRODIE

The outlet of the Mararoa River by the swing-bridge at South Mavora was used to portray the junction of the *Silverlode* and *Anduin Rivers* as the Fellowship left *Lothlórien*.

Brown and rainbow trout abound in the river and provide another ready source of food for the barbecue, provided, of course, you've remembered to organise a fishing licence. Because of the tranquillity a population of bush robins reside nearby and New Zealand falcons are often seen soaring in the thermals overhead.

For those not wishing to try a camping lifestyle there are a number of tourist operators based in Queenstown and Te Anau offering 4WD day trips into the area. Queenstown company Heliworks also offer helicopter flights over these locations. The nearby village of Mossburn offers farm-stay accommodation and can be used as a base for a day trip into the area. The town of Te Anau is only 45 minutes by car and can also be used as your local touring headquarters.

Tolkien's *Silverlode* was a fair river flowing from its source in *Nanduhirion* through *Lórien* and on into the great *Anduin River*. The pristine beauty of the Mararoa River as it leaves the South Mavora certainly brings his description vividly to mind, in a tranquil and profoundly beautiful location.

IAN BRODIE

Opposite top: Mavora Lakes with the edge of Fangorn Forest.

Opposite bottom: Mooring place at Nen Hithoel.

Above top: South Mavora Lake from the Mararoa River outlet.

Above: View from the campsite at Amon Hen.

an introduction

IAN BRODIE

Above: Lake Te Anau.

Below: Early morning fog on Lake Te Anau.

Opposite: The edge of Fangorn Forest (Takaro Road).

Gateway to Fiordland National Park, the township of Te Anau sits beside one of the most splendid lakes in New Zealand. As you stand on the lakefront the brooding bush-covered foothills, draw your eye skywards to towering peaks, and it's easy to understand why this area was chosen to portray the mountainous realms of Middle-earth.

The second largest lake in New Zealand, Lake Te Anau covers 43,200 ha and is over 417 m in depth.

Allow at least three days to fully experience some spectacular journeys including Milford Sound, Doubtful Sound and the Te Ana-au Caves.

Milford Sound is the easiest and most accessible fiord in New Zealand and each year thousands of tourist drive, fly or walk into the area. A popular choice is the fly/drive option, allowing visitors to see the famed Milford Track, Sutherland Falls (one of the worlds highest at 580.3 m) and Sound from the air. After landing at the small airfield a number of cruise options out to the open sea are available. The view from the mouth is stunning, with the return by coach equally impressive, stopping at the Chasm (where the Cleddau River has carved its way through solid rock) and the Homer Tunnel.

A visit to the Redcliff Bar & Café comes highly recommended. During filming in the area, the stars frequented the café and part-owner Megan Harvey has an autographed T-shirt to prove it. One evening dinner coincided with poetry-reading night. After various recitations a deep voice resounded, reciting a Shakespearian sonnet. The reading finished, the visitors applauded and John Rhys Davies took a deep bow and left.

IAN BRODIE

INTERNET
www.fiordland.org.nz

Fangorn Forest

IAN BRODIE

A wonderful bush location is situated on Takaro Road. Leaving Te Anau on the main Queenstown highway, turn left onto Kakapo Road just a few kilometres from town. Travel down this road approximately 9 km and turn left onto Takaro Road. After a further 6 km the unsealed road passes through a delightful bushy glade with an unnamed access road on the left.

Park in the little turning area. Filming was undertaken on both sides of the road to portray *Fangorn Forest* with remote cameras strung from high wires to capture *Aragorn* moving through the trees. This lovely forest of red and silver beech seems untouched for millions of years while the forest floor is carpeted with moss of the most intense green.

Beech trees are pollinated by pollen grains caught by the wind. After fertilisation beech flowers produce seeds in the form of small 'nuts'. The seeds rarely blow more than a few metres before falling to the forest floor where they germinate and grow in the shade of the parent tree. The half-light of the forest floor stunts the young seedlings' growth, until a mature tree falls to the ground allowing light to flood in. Once established the trees can grow up to 30 m tall and live for more than 300 years.

PIERRE VINET

So it was literally going to another world, a world of clean air, the most crystal-clear water, and the richest of green in the trees. There are these huge, towering summits and volcanoes, and rivers and streams. It's like Tolkien walked across New Zealand and then sat down to write the trilogy.

Sean Astin

FANGORN FOREST
S45° 21" 087—E167° 54" 477

IAN BRODIE

PIERRE VINET

Tolkien was writing about a different world, a different land, a primitive land and a primitive time in history. New Zealand — breathtakingly beautiful — is just perfect for that.

John Rhys-Davies

IAN BRODIE

Flowing from Lake Te Anau to Lake Manapouri, the Waiau River was used to portray parts of the majestic *River Anduin*. Bush-clad banks perfectly set the scene illustrating the first part of the river journey undertaken by the Fellowship before they reached the *Brown lands*, the desolate and treeless area between *Mirkwood* and the *Emyn Muil*, where long ago the *Ent Wives* made their gardens. Sections of the river are accessible from the main Te Anau – Manapouri road and the entire waterway can be viewed on the longer of the three different Heliworks' helicopter tour options from Queenstown.

A more energetic option for the hale and hearty is to undertake the 67-km Kepler Track, commencing in Te Anau. A reasonable level of fitness is required to complete the full tramp over three to four days, which traverses lake edges, beech forests, mountain-tops and a U-shaped glacial valley, and provides a more personal appreciation of our heroes' journey!

For those with less time take the main Te Anau / Manapouri highway and turn right at the DOC Rainbow Reach sign. As the unsealed road first veers left (and before it veers right again) turn right down the unmarked track. A magnificent view of the *River Anduin* can be obtained from this viewpoint. If you continue a further 2 km down the access road there is a swing bridge across the river and the opportunity to take a shorter walk on the Kepler Track. The journey is 10.9 km one way but even a short stroll will take you into the native beech forest and provide beautiful views of the river. More information on the Kepler Track can be obtained from the local DOC Headquarters in Te Anau.

RIVER ANDUIN VIEWPOINT
S45° 29' 755—E167° 40' 159

Situated 12 km from Te Anau, Lake Manapouri (lake of the sorrowing heart) is an area of unspoilt beauty, and the island-studded blue lake and bush-covered Kepler Mountains invite closer exploration.

While filming, unpredictable weather delivered an unseasonable November snowfall. Huge wet snowflakes began to settle on the ground and cover the

IAN BRODIE

poor Hobbits. Showing no sign of dissipating, when the snow was over 20 cm deep the cast and crew quickly decided to change scenes to the local Manapouri Hall.

One of the best ways to explore the area is to take the full-day Doubtful Sound excursion with Fiordland Travel. Commencing with a cruise across the lake, the journey continues by bus over the Wilmot Pass (670.9 m) and culminates with a three-hour boat cruise to the sea on Doubtful Sound. Three times longer than Milford Sound and with a surface area ten times larger, Doubtful Sound is home to a resident pod of about 60 bottlenose dolphins and New Zealand fur seals can be seen basking on the rocks at the Nee Islets. Scattered around the sound is the rare and very shy Fiordland crested penguin.

Over millions of years the collision of rock and ice has sculpted this landscape, now cloaked in dense cool temperate rainforest. The 'sound of silence' and complete isolation as one cruises the sound is one of its many charms.

On the journey across Lake Manapouri cast your eyes upwards to the high mountaintops on your right, by Freeman Burn. Situated far up in these alpine peaks are the Norwest Lakes — locations used to show the Fellowship heading south from *Rivendell*.

IAN BRODIE

Opposite top: Waiau River from a viewpoint near the Kepler Track.

Opposite bottom: The Kepler Track.

Above top: Lake Manapouri, looking towards the rough country south of Rivendell.

Above bottom: Pearl Harbour, starting point for the Doubtful Sound excursion.

IAN BRODIE

Above and below: Norwest Lakes are a remote and beautiful location.

Opposite top and bottom left: Aerial views of the area used to film *Arwen's* flight.

Opposite middle left: Norwest Lakes on a perfect autumn day.

Opposite middle right: The area used to show the Fellowship heading south, through Eregion.

Opposite bottom right: A Heliworks Squirrel helicopter perched in the remote Norwest Lakes area.

The helicopter is no stranger to this part of the world; in the 1960s it became the 'mount' for commercial deer hunters, who combed the area for prize venison. Commercial hunting gave way to farming but the helicopter remains and now serves as the perfect transportation for reaching the more remote locations.

As the ring heads south a wild and rugged land opens in front of the Fellowship and perched high in the Kepler Mountains, the Norwest Lakes are closely reminiscent of Middle-earth.

The opening sequence of the *Flight to the Ford* showing *Arwen* and *Frodo* in the desperate escape from the *Black Riders* was also filmed near Te Anau. The location is only accessible on the longer Heliworks' helicopter tour.

IAN BRODIE

IAN BRODIE

IAN BRODIE

IAN BRODIE

IAN BRODIE

IAN BRODIE

PIERRE VINET

Above: Orcs on the rampage in Rohan.

Below: A rebuilt Chinese miner's cottage near Poolburn.

Opposite top: The green and rolling hills of Rohan were gifted to the Rohirrim by Cirion of Gondor in TA2510.

Opposite bottom: Wind erosion on schist has created marvellous shapes.

The cycle of the seasons are more apparent in Central Otago than anywhere else in New Zealand. In summer temperatures exceed 30°C and the hills shimmer in the burning heat; in winter temperatures as low as –15°C cover the trees in ghostly white hoar frost. In autumn the region becomes a sea of gold as poplars and willows prepare for winter; in spring fruit trees welcome the warmer weather with a stunning blossom display.

The lure of gold in 1862 brought people to the region. As the easily won gold was soon depleted the population decreased, until the 1890s, when the idea of dredging for gold saw a resurgence in population of nearby Alexandra.

When the dredging began to dwindle, residents discovered the soil was rich in potash and phosphoric acid and fruit orchards became the new gold.

The township of Clyde still has a number of original buildings from the 1800s, serving wonderful food incorporating the best in local produce.

Alexandra is the main service town for the Central Otago Region and has a number of attractions related to the gold discoveries. Very popular in summer, it has the distinction of the lowest rainfall of any town in New Zealand.

A great way to explore this region is via the Central Otago Rail Trail. Although the trains have now gone, 150 km of track from Clyde to Middlemarch has been converted into a trail for bikes, horses or pedestrians. While easily accessible from the road for a day trip, to really savour the spectacular scenery, consider hiring a cycle and stopping overnight at one of the small country hotels en-route.

IAN BRODIE

INTERNET

www.tco.org.nz

Rohan

The area surrounding the Poolburn Reservoir high on the Rough Ridge Range in the Ida Valley was used extensively to portray *Rohan*. It was the perfect choice, as the rolling hills with distinctive rocky tors and expansive vistas invite comparison with the realm of the *Riddermark*.

PIERRE VINET

Poolburn Reservoir is remote and the rough road from the valley floor is recommended for four-wheel-drive vehicles only. It is also very exposed and care should be taken; the weather can change quickly with snow possible during three seasons.

The cast and crew spent many weeks filming at Poolburn, staying at a number of localities including Alexandra and Cromwell. Due to the condition of the access road they met at the foot of the hill and were transported up by 4WD. This resulted in very long days, often starting at 5 a.m. and finishing at 8 p.m.

Situated an impressive 40-minute drive from Alexandra, the sealed drive to the foot of the ranges takes you to the village of Omakau, where the nearby racecourse was used as the production office. Take a right turn into the small hamlet of Ophir. Gold was discovered in 1863, and Ophir was named after the biblical realm where the Queen of Sheba obtained gold for King Solomon.

The road now climbs across the Raggedy Range, with wonderful views from the summit of a land seemingly untouched by humans. The sky is usually an intense blue and in summer the shimmering heat haze seems to distort distances into a golden sphere. After descending to the valley floor turn right at the Poolburn Hotel onto Moa Creek Road and continue on to Webster Lane, where you need to turn left into the unpaved road.

The climb to Poolburn itself commences beside Bonspiel Station, and for those without appropriate vehicles, it is a logical stopping space. The local landowners organise tours of Poolburn in their 4WD and as many of the locations were situated on their property they are the ideal hosts to take you to *Rohan*. They also have home-stay accommodation available in original Chinese miners' huts.

IAN BRODIE

Rohan

IAN BRODIE

Above: Poolburn's fishing huts were camouflaged as farmhouses.

Below: The Orcs' plundering of the small Rohirrim village would be avenged at the Battle of Helm's Deep.

Poolburn Dam was completed in 1931, as a storage lake to irrigate the Ida Valley below. The land is rich and during the height of the gold rush there were five hotels dispensing liquid warmth to miners toiling in the harsh environment. Today it's a popular recreational area and the reservoir is richly stocked with brown trout.

On reaching the lake, there is an excellent view across to the location of the small village where *Morwen* sent her children to safety before attack. No trace of the village remains but the area is immediately recognisable.

A number of other sites were used in this locality to show the Hobbits being rushed to *Saruman* and the epic chase by *Aragorn*, *Gimli* and *Legolas*.

PIERRE VINET

VIEWPOINT OF *ROHIRRIM* VILLAGE: S45° 17.769—E169° 44.346
LOCATION OF POOLBURN UNIT BASE: S45° 17.610—E 169°43.623

For a voyage of discovery through Middle-earth New Zealand the following sixteen-day itinerary includes most of the important locations.

PIERRE VINET

Day One: Auckland – Matamata – Taupo
▷ *Hobbiton*

Day Two: Taupo – The Chateau

Day Three: The Chateau
▷ *Mordor*

Day Four: The Chateau – Otaki
▷ *River Anduin*

Day Five: Otaki – Wellington
▷ *Leaving The Shire*

Day Six: Wellington
▷ *Leaving The Shire*
▷ *Embassy Theatre*
▷ *Chocolate Fish Café*

Day Seven: Wellington
▷ *River Anduin*
▷ *Rivendell*
▷ *Isengard Gardens*

Day Eight: Wellington – Nelson
▷ *Artisans*

Everything here is more magnificent. The landscape is familiar in the sense it's been formed by rain — just as Tolkien's Oxfordshire was — but the vegetation is unusual and the mountains seem so much sharper. If you're looking for what the poets used to call 'the awful' — a sense of awe — that is what you find in New Zealand. And it's wild in a way that England isn't wild.

Ian McKellen

TOTALLY WELLINGTON

PIERRE VINET

We did everything – bungy jumping, surfing, motorcycle riding, we did it all. Sightseeing, taking in the America's Cup regatta – we were the Fellowship around town in New Zealand.

Sean Astin

PIERRE VINET

The woods were nearby. A beautiful river was always nearby. No matter how urban a place was, it was never very far away from something that felt more or less primeval.

Viggo Mortensen

Day Nine: Nelson
  ▷ *Chetwood Forest*
  ▷ *Rough Country South of Rivendell*
  ▷ *Dimrill Dale*

Day Ten: Nelson – Methven

Day Eleven: Methven – Wanaka
  ▷ *Edoras*
  ▷ *Flight to the Ford*
  ▷ *Rough Country South of Rivendell*

Day Twelve: Wanaka – Glenorchy
  ▷ *Pillars of the Argonath*
  ▷ *Ford of Bruinen*
  ▷ *Amon Hen*
  ▷ *Ithilien Camp*

Day Thirteen: Glenorchy – Queenstown
  ▷ *Isengard*
  ▷ *Lothlórien*
  ▷ *Amon Hen*

Day Fourteen: Queenstown
  ▷ *Deer Park Heights*
  ▷ *Dimrill Dale*

Day Fifteen: Queenstown – Mavora Lakes – Te Anau
  ▷ *Amon Hen*
  ▷ *Fangorn Forest*

Day Sixteen: Te Anau
  ▷ *River Anduin*

PIERRE VINET

A

Abel Tasman National Park **46**, 48
A.J. Hackett Bungy 60
Alexandra 88, 89
Amon Hen 15, 41, 59, 62, 67, 69, **72**, 74, 76, **77**, 78, 81, 92
Amon Lhâw 72
Amon Sûl 13
Arizona Bar & Grill 42, 43
Arrow River 63, **64**, 66, 78
Arrowtown 62, **63**, 78
Arthur's Point 78
Ashburton Gorge 53
Auckland 17, 30, 91

B

Bag End 12, **18**, **19**
Black Gate (The) 73
Blue Mountains (The) 56
Bob's Peak 67
Brava 43
Brown Lands (The) 84
Bree 12, **44**, 48

C

Canaan Road 48
Canterbury Plains 53
Caradhras **12**
Cardrona Hotel 57
Cardrona River 57
Cardrona Ski field 57
Cardrona Valley 57
Celebrant see River Celebrant
Central Otago Rail Trail 88
Chard Farm 61, 78
Chetwood Forest **48**, 49, 92
Chocolate Fish Café 42, **43**
Cleddau River 82
Closeburn 67, **72**, 73
Clutha River 56, 62
Clyde 88
Cook Strait 32
Coronet Peak 65

Cromwell 56, 61, 62, 78
Crown Range 57, 58, 62

D

Dagorlad Plain 23
Dan's Paddock 75
Dart / Rees Track 74
Dart River **74**, 76
Dart River Safaris 75, **76**
Dart Stables 75, 77
Dead Marshes (The) 15
Deeping Comb 15
Deeping Tower 45
Deeping Wall 45
Deer Park Heights **68**, 78
Diamond Lake 75
Dimrill Dale 59, **69**, **70**, 78, 92
Dimrill Gate 70
Dol Amroth 62
Doubtful Sound 82, 85
Dunland 49
Dry Creek Quarry 42
Dymocks Booksellers 31

E

Earnslaw (The) 67
Edoras 15, **53**, **54**, **55**, 92
Embassy Cinema 31, 42, 91
Emyn Muil 13, 15
Erewhon **53**,
Eriador **44**, 79
Eregion **50**, **57**, **59**, **86**, **87**
Ethir Anduin 62
Ettenmoors 27
Extreme Green Rafting 62

F

Falls of Rauros 72
Fangorn Forest 78, **79**, **80**, 83, 92
Featherston 34, 35
Fell Museum 35
Fernside 36
Film Centre (The) 31

Fiordland National Park   82
Five Rivers   79
Ford of Bruinen   56, 59, 62, **64, 65,** 69, 78, **87,** 92
Ford of Rivendell   see Ford of Bruinen
Fords of Isen   38
Fort Dorset   13, 44
Foxton   27
Freeman Burn   85

G

Gibbston Valley Wines   61, 78
Glendhu Bay   57, **59**
Glenorchy   72, **74,** 76, 77, 92
Glen Roydon Lodge   74
Gladden Fields   **36**
Glittering Caves   45
Goldfields Mining Centre   62
Gondor   61, 62, 68, 72, 73, 75, 88
Grand Chateau   22, 23, 25, 91
Great East Road (The)   **56,** 64, **87**
Green Parrot (The)   43
Greenstone Track   74
Grey Havens (The)   56

H

Hamilton   18
Harad   25, 73
Harcourt Park   **39, 40,** 42
Harrington Brewers   47
Harward's Hole   48
Hawea   56
Hawea Flat   57
Hayward's Hill   42, 45
Heliworks   69, 70, 78, 81, 84, 86, **87**
Helm's Deep   31, 42, 45
Helm's Gate   45, 90
Henneth Annûn   22, 25
Hightime Bungy   **26,**
Hobbiton   12, **18,** 44, 47, 91
Homer Tunnel   82
Hornburg   45
Hutt River   **37,** 38, 40, **41,** 42
Hutt Valley   34, 37

I

Ida Valley   89, 90
Imladris   see Rivendell
Isengard   **39, 40,** 42, 57, **75,** 76, 78, 91, 92
Ithilien   **27**
Ithilien Camp   25, 27, **73,** 92
Iwikau Village   23

K

Kahurangi National Park   46, 49, 51
Kaiteriteri   48
Kaitoke Regional Park   13, **16,** 29, **37, 38,** 39, 42
Kakapo Road   83
Kapiti Coast   27
Kawarau Gorge   62
Kawarau River   60, **61,** 62, 68, 78
Kelvin Heights   68
Kepler Mountains   85, 86
Kepler Track   84
Kingston   67

L

Lambton Quay   30
Lake Alta   **67,** 69, **70,**
Lake Camp   53
Lake Clearwater   53
Lake Dunstan   62
Lake Hawea   *see Hawea*
Lake Hayes   **63,** 78
Lake Manapouri   *see Manapouri*
Lake Te Anau   *see Te Anau*
Lake Wakatipu   13, 62, **66,** 67, 72, 74
Lake Wanaka   *see Wanaka*
Lakes District Museum   63
Lighthouse Cinema (The)   37
Lindis Pass (The)   56
Lindon   56
Lothlórien   12, 15, 35, **36,** 62, 69, 70, 74, 75, **76,** 77, **78,** 81, 92
Lyall Bay   43

M

Manapouri   84, **85**
Mangaweka   26